Wicca's Book of Crystal Spells

Madame Ophelia

Copyright © 2023 by Madame Ophelia

All rights reserved.

No portion of this book may be reproduced in any form without written permission from the publisher or author, except as permitted by U.S. copyright law.

Contents

1. Introduction — 1
2. Brief overview of Wicca and its connection to crystals — 3
3. Importance of crystal spells in Wiccan practice — 6
4. How this book will guide readers in incorporating crystals into their magical workings — 9
5. Understanding Crystals in Wicca — 12
6. Choosing the right crystals for different intentions and spells — 16
7. Cleansing and charging crystals for optimal spellwork — 20
8. Crystal Spellcrafting Basics — 24
9. Setting up a sacred space for crystal magic — 28
10. Casting circles and invoking elemental energies — 32

11. Crafting and consecrating ritual tools for crystal spells — 36

12. Crystal Spells for Love and Relationships — 40

13. Attracting love and enhancing romantic relationships with crystals — 43

14. Healing and restoring harmony in troubled relationships — 46

15. Strengthening bonds and promoting self-love using crystal magic — 50

16. Crystal Spells for Protection and Cleansing — 53

17. Creating crystal amulets and talismans for personal protection — 57

18. Shielding and warding spells with crystals for home and sacred spaces — 60

19. Clearing negative energies and purifying spaces with crystal grids — 63

20. Crystal Spells for Healing and Well-being — 66

21. Utilizing crystals for physical healing and pain relief — 71

22. Enhancing emotional well-being and releasing negative patterns — 74

23. Promoting spiritual growth and connecting with higher consciousness using crystals — 77

24.	Crystal Spells for Abundance and Prosperity	81
25.	Manifesting abundance and attracting financial prosperity with crystals	84
26.	Using crystals for career success and manifestation of goals	87
27.	Cultivating gratitude and abundance mindset through crystal magic	90
28.	Crystal Spells for Divination and Intuition	93
29.	Strengthening psychic abilities and intuition with crystal rituals	97
30.	Crystal scrying and crystal pendulum for divination purposes	101
31.	Enhancing dreamwork and astral projection using crystals	105
32.	Crystal Spells for Rituals and Sabbats	109
33.	Incorporating crystals into Wiccan rituals and celebrations	113
34.	Crystal spells for each of the eight Sabbats in the Wheel of the Year	116
35.	Aligning with seasonal energies and enhancing magical potency with crystals	120
36.	Conclusion	124

37. Recap of the importance of crystal spells in Wicca — 126
38. Encouragement for readers to explore and experiment with their own crystal magic — 129
39. Final thoughts on the transformative power of crystals in spiritual practice — 132

Chapter 1

Introduction

WELCOME TO "WICCA'S BOOK of Crystal Spells," a guide dedicated to exploring the enchanting world of crystal magic within the framework of Wiccan practice. In this book, we will embark on a journey to discover the profound connection between Wicca and the power of crystals.

Wicca, a modern pagan religion rooted in ancient traditions, embraces a harmonious relationship with nature and the divine. Central to Wiccan belief is the understanding that energy permeates everything around us, and harnessing this energy enables us to create positive change in our lives. Crystals, with their unique energetic properties, have long been regarded as potent tools for spellcasting and spiritual transformation.

This book serves as your key to unlocking the magic within crystals and integrating them seamlessly into your Wiccan spellcraft. Whether you are a novice practitioner or an experienced witch, the knowledge and practices shared here will deepen your understanding of crystal spells and enhance your magical workings.

Throughout these pages, we will delve into the fundamental principles of working with crystals in Wiccan rituals and spells. We will explore how to choose the right crystals for specific intentions, how to cleanse and charge them effectively, and how to create a sacred space conducive to magical workings.

The chapters that follow will cover various aspects of life where crystal spells can be employed. We will delve into spells for love and relationships, protection and cleansing, healing and well-being, abundance and prosperity, divination and intuition, as well as their integration into rituals and Sabbats throughout the Wheel of the Year.

By incorporating crystal magic into your Wiccan practice, you will open up new avenues of personal growth, spiritual connection, and manifestation. Each spell, ritual, and technique shared in this book has been carefully crafted to empower you on your magical journey.

Remember, the power lies within you, and the crystals are the conduits to manifest that power. Embrace the wisdom of the Earth, the energy of the universe, and the sacred teachings of Wicca as we embark on this transformative exploration of crystal spells.

May this book inspire and guide you to unlock the enchanting possibilities that await when Wicca and crystals intertwine in harmonious synergy.

Chapter 2

Brief overview of Wicca and its connection to crystals

WICCA IS A MODERN pagan religion that draws inspiration from ancient practices and beliefs. Rooted in reverence for nature, Wicca embraces a spiritual path that honors the cycles of the seasons, the divine feminine and masculine, and the interconnectedness of all living things. It celebrates a deep connection with the Earth and seeks to harness natural energies for personal and collective transformation.

Crystals play a significant role in Wiccan practice, serving as powerful tools for energy work, spellcraft, and spiritual growth. Wiccans believe that crystals possess unique energetic properties that can be utilized to enhance magical intentions and manifestations. These properties arise from the crystalline structures of minerals and the specific vibrations they emit.

Wiccans often align particular crystals with corresponding intentions or energies. For example, clear quartz is commonly associated with clarity, amplification, and spiritual connection, while amethyst is linked to psychic abilities and spiritual protection.

Each crystal is believed to carry its own distinct energy signature that can be harnessed to amplify intentions and support magical workings.

Crystals are cleansed and charged to align them with the practitioner's intentions and to clear any residual energies they may carry. Wiccans employ various methods such as moonlight bathing, sunlight exposure, smudging with herbs, and placing them on sacred altars or crystal grids for purification and recharging.

In Wiccan rituals, crystals are often used to create sacred space, establish energetic boundaries, and invoke specific elemental energies. They can be incorporated into spellwork through placement on altars, carried as charms or amulets, or used in crystal grids to amplify and direct energy. Wiccans also utilize crystals for divination, scrying, and enhancing intuition.

The connection between Wicca and crystals extends beyond mere tools for magic. Wiccans view crystals as living entities with their own consciousness and energies. They cultivate a respectful relationship with crystals, recognizing them as allies in their spiritual journey and co-creators in their magical manifestations.

In the realm of Wicca, crystals are regarded as conduits of Earth's wisdom and elemental energies, helping practitioners attune to the natural rhythms of the universe and align with their own inner power. The integration of crystals into Wiccan practice deepens the connection with the Earth, enhances magical potency, and facilitates spiritual growth.

Throughout this book, we will explore the multifaceted ways in which Wiccans utilize crystals in their spells, rituals, and daily practice. By tapping into the profound relationship between Wicca and crystals, we can unlock the transformative magic they hold and harness their energy for our own spiritual evolution.

Chapter 3

Importance of crystal spells in Wiccan practice

CRYSTAL SPELLS HOLD A significant role in Wiccan practice, serving as potent tools for intention setting, energy manipulation, and spiritual transformation. Here are some key reasons for the importance of crystal spells in Wicca:

1. Amplifying Intentions: Crystals possess unique energetic vibrations that can amplify and enhance the intentions set by a practitioner. When combined with focused intention and spellwork, crystals act as powerful conduits, magnifying the energy directed toward a specific goal or desire. They help to align the practitioner's energy with their desired outcome, increasing the effectiveness of their magical workings.

2. Connecting with Earth's Energies: Wicca emphasizes the sacredness of nature and the interconnectedness of all living things. Crystals, being formed within the Earth over millions of years, carry the energies and wisdom of

the natural world. By working with crystals, Wiccans establish a deep connection with the Earth's energies, aligning themselves with the cycles of nature and tapping into its abundant and transformative power.

3. Enhancing Rituals and Spellcraft: Crystals are utilized in Wiccan rituals and spellcraft to create sacred space, direct energy, and strengthen the effectiveness of magical workings. They can be placed on altars, incorporated into spell components, or arranged in crystal grids to focus and direct energy. Crystals serve as energetic anchors, helping to ground and center the practitioner during ritual and spellcasting, thus heightening their focus and intention.

4. Promoting Balance and Healing: Crystals are renowned for their healing properties, both on a physical and energetic level. In Wiccan practice, crystals are utilized to restore balance, promote well-being, and facilitate inner healing. They can be used in rituals and spells to support emotional healing, relieve physical ailments, and restore harmony to the mind, body, and spirit.

5. Deepening Spiritual Connection: Wicca is a spiritual path that encourages the exploration and cultivation of a personal connection with the divine. Crystals aid in deepening this connection by serving as tools for meditation, prayer, and spiritual attunement. They can help

to quiet the mind, open the heart, and facilitate a greater sense of spiritual awareness, allowing practitioners to connect with their higher selves and the divine realms.

6. Facilitating Divination and Intuition: Crystals have long been associated with enhancing psychic abilities and intuition. In Wiccan practice, crystals are used for divination purposes, such as scrying or crystal gazing, as well as for developing and honing intuitive abilities. By working with specific crystals, practitioners can access higher realms of consciousness, gain insights, and receive guidance in their magical and spiritual journeys.

In summary, crystal spells play a vital role in Wiccan practice, enabling practitioners to harness the Earth's energies, amplify intentions, enhance rituals, promote healing, deepen spiritual connection, and facilitate intuitive and divinatory abilities. By embracing the power of crystals, Wiccans tap into the transformative potential of these natural allies, enriching their magical practice and spiritual growth.

Chapter 4

How this book will guide readers in incorporating crystals into their magical workings

IN "WICCA'S BOOK OF Crystal Spells," readers will find a comprehensive and practical guide to incorporating crystals into their magical workings within the framework of Wiccan practice. This book is designed to provide step-by-step guidance and empower readers to harness the transformative power of crystals. Here's how this book will guide readers:

1. Understanding Crystal Properties: The book begins by introducing readers to the energetic properties of crystals. It explains how different crystals resonate with specific intentions, energies, and chakras. Readers will gain a deep understanding of how to choose the right crystals for their magical workings based on their unique properties.

2. Cleansing and Charging Crystals: Effective cleansing and charging methods are essential to ensure that crys-

tals are clear of any stagnant or unwanted energies and are aligned with the practitioner's intentions. This book offers various techniques for cleansing and charging crystals, including moonlight bathing, sunlight exposure, using elemental energies, and invoking ritual purification.

3. Creating a Sacred Space: A sacred space is crucial for effective magical workings. Readers will learn how to set up and consecrate their sacred space, whether it's a dedicated altar or a specific area for ritual and spellcraft. The book provides guidance on incorporating crystals into the sacred space to amplify and enhance its energy.

4. Spellcrafting with Crystals: This book offers a wide range of crystal spells for different purposes, such as love and relationships, protection and cleansing, healing and well-being, abundance and prosperity, divination and intuition, and more. Each spell is accompanied by clear instructions, including the crystals to be used, the step-by-step process, and suggestions for maximizing the spell's effectiveness.

5. Rituals and Techniques: Readers will discover various rituals and techniques that incorporate crystals into their magical practice. These include crystal grids, where specific crystals are arranged in a geometric pattern to amplify intentions; crystal elixirs and potions,

which infuse the energy of crystals into liquid form for consumption or topical use; and working with crystal pendulums for divination and energy clearing.

6. Integrating Crystals into Sabbats and Ritual Celebrations: This book explores how to integrate crystals into Wiccan Sabbats and ritual celebrations throughout the Wheel of the Year. Readers will find specific crystal spells and rituals tailored to each Sabbat, allowing them to harness the seasonal energies and deepen their connection with the cycles of nature.

Throughout the book, there will be practical tips, precautions, and guidance on working with crystals ethically and responsibly. The aim is to empower readers to develop their intuitive connection with crystals and adapt the spells and techniques to their personal needs and preferences.

By the end of the book, readers will have gained the knowledge, confidence, and practical skills to incorporate crystals seamlessly into their magical workings. They will be able to infuse their Wiccan practice with the transformative power of crystals, enhancing their spellcraft, deepening their spiritual connection, and experiencing the profound magic that arises when Wicca and crystals converge.

Chapter 5

Understanding Crystals in Wicca

Exploring the Energetic Properties of Crystals

1. Crystal Formation and Composition: This section provides an overview of how crystals are formed and their diverse chemical compositions. It explains how these factors contribute to the unique energetic properties of each crystal.

2. Vibrational Frequencies: Crystals are known for their vibrational frequencies, which affect the energy they emit. Readers will learn about the concept of vibrational resonance and how it relates to working with crystals in spellcasting and energy work.

3. Crystal Structures and Correspondences: Different crystals have distinct geometric structures, which influence their metaphysical properties. This section explores various crystal structures and their correspondences to specific intentions, chakras, elements, and as-

trological signs.

B. Choosing the Right Crystals for Different Intentions and Spells

   1. Crystal Selection Guidelines: Readers will discover practical tips and considerations for choosing the most appropriate crystals for their magical workings. They will learn to assess the color, shape, energetic properties, and intuitive resonance of crystals when selecting them for specific intentions.

   2. Crystal Associations and Correspondences: This section presents a comprehensive reference guide to the energetic correspondences of crystals. It explores associations with specific intentions, magical workings, deities, elements, planets, and zodiac signs, allowing readers to align their intentions with the suitable crystals.

   3. Crystal Combinations and Pairings: Understanding how different crystals interact with one another is crucial in spellcasting. Readers will learn about crystal combinations that enhance each other's energies and create synergistic effects, enabling them to design more potent and focused spells.

C. Cleansing and Charging Crystals for Optimal Spellwork
   1. Importance of Cleansing Crystals: Before utilizing

crystals in spells, it is essential to cleanse them of any residual energies. This section explores various cleansing methods, including moonlight, sunlight, water, smoke, sound, and intention-based techniques, empowering readers to select the most suitable cleansing method for their crystals.

2. Charging Crystals with Intention: Charging crystals infuses them with focused energy aligned with the desired intention. Readers will learn techniques for charging crystals, such as visualization, intention-setting rituals, elemental energy infusion, and working with lunar or solar energies.

3. Programming and Attuning Crystals: Programming crystals involves directing their energies towards specific goals or intentions. This section covers methods for programming crystals, including visualization, affirmations, and meditation, enabling readers to establish a strong energetic connection with their chosen crystals.

By delving into the understanding of crystals in Wicca, readers will gain a solid foundation in working with these powerful tools. They will be equipped with the knowledge needed to select the appropriate crystals for their magical intentions, cleanse and charge them effectively, and attune their energy for optimal spellwork. Understanding the energetic properties of crystals opens the doorway to their transformative potential in Wiccan practice.

Chapter 6

Choosing the right crystals for different intentions and spells

1. Understanding Intention: Before selecting crystals for a particular spell or intention, it is crucial to have a clear understanding of the desired outcome. Take time to reflect on the purpose of the spell and the specific energies you wish to invoke or manifest.

2. Researching Crystal Properties: Familiarize yourself with the energetic properties and correspondences of different crystals. Consult reference materials, crystal guides, or reputable online sources to explore the metaphysical properties, colors, shapes, and associated chakras or elements of various crystals.

3. Intuitive Connection: Trust your intuition when choosing crystals. Allow yourself to be drawn to certain crystals that resonate with your intention. Pay attention

to any physical or energetic sensations you may experience when holding or interacting with a crystal. Trust your instincts and select the crystals that feel right for your purpose.

4. Specific Intentions and Associations: Consider the specific intentions or aspects you want to address in your spell. Match those intentions with the correspondences and properties of crystals. For example:

- Love and Relationships: Crystals like rose quartz, rhodonite, and emerald are often associated with love, compassion, and harmonious relationships.

- Protection and Cleansing: Black tourmaline, smoky quartz, and obsidian are commonly used for grounding, protection, and clearing negative energies.

- Healing and Well-being: Amethyst, clear quartz, and green aventurine are known for their healing properties and can be used for physical, emotional, or spiritual healing.

- Abundance and Prosperity: Citrine, pyrite, and green jade are often used to attract abundance, prosperity, and good fortune.

- Intuition and Divination: Labradorite, amethyst, and moonstone are popular choices for enhancing psychic abilities, intuition, and accessing higher realms of consciousness.

1. Crystal Combinations: Experiment with combining different crystals to amplify their energies or create a harmonious blend for your intention. Some crystals work synergistically, enhancing each other's properties. For example, combining amethyst and clear quartz can amplify spiritual awareness and intuition.

2. Personal Preferences: Consider your personal connection and affinity for certain crystals. You may have a natural attraction or resonance with particular crystals, which can enhance your energetic bond and effectiveness in spellcasting.

3. Accessibility and Availability: Take into account the availability and accessibility of crystals in your area. While certain crystals may be ideal for your intention, it's important to work with what is accessible to you. Explore local crystal shops, online retailers, or crystal fairs to find the crystals that align with your intentions.

Remember that there are no hard and fast rules when it comes to selecting crystals. Trust your intuition, explore correspondences, and experiment with different combinations to find the crystals that resonate with your unique magical practice. Ultimately, the most important factor is your own connection and intention when working with crystals in Wiccan spells and rituals.

Chapter 7

Cleansing and charging crystals for optimal spellwork

1. Importance of Cleansing: Cleansing crystals is a crucial step before using them in spellwork. Crystals can absorb and hold onto various energies, both positive and negative, which may interfere with their effectiveness. Cleansing clears away any unwanted energies, allowing the crystal to resonate with your intention.

2. Selecting a Cleansing Method: There are several methods to cleanse crystals, and you can choose the one that resonates with you or the specific crystal. Here are some commonly used cleansing techniques:

    - Moonlight Cleansing: Place your crystals outdoors or by a windowsill during a full moon or a specific moon phase that aligns with your intention. Allow the moonlight to cleanse and recharge the crystals' energy.

- Sunlight Cleansing: Some crystals can be cleansed in sunlight, but be mindful as prolonged exposure to sunlight may fade or damage certain crystals. Use this method selectively, considering the properties of the crystal.

- Elemental Cleansing: Use the elements of earth, air, water, or fire to cleanse your crystals. You can bury them in the earth for a period of time, pass them through incense smoke, rinse them in flowing water, or lightly pass them over a candle flame while visualizing the cleansing process.

- Sound Cleansing: Use sound vibrations to cleanse crystals by placing them near a singing bowl, using a tuning fork, or using other sound instruments. The vibrations help dislodge and release any stagnant energies held within the crystals.

- Intention Cleansing: Hold the crystal in your hands and set the intention that it be cleansed of all previous energies. Visualize pure, vibrant light surrounding and permeating the crystal, purifying it completely.

- Smudging: Pass your crystals through the smoke of

sacred herbs such as sage, palo santo, or cedar. The smoke helps remove negative energies, purifying the crystal.

3. Charging Methods: Charging crystals aligns them with your intention and activates their energy for optimal spellwork. Consider the following charging techniques:

- Moonlight Charging: Similar to moonlight cleansing, you can place your crystals in moonlight during a specific moon phase that corresponds to your intention. Set the intention that the moon's energy charges and empowers the crystals.

- Sunlight Charging: If the crystal can tolerate sunlight, place it in direct sunlight for a short duration, setting the intention that the solar energy infuses the crystal with power and vitality.

- Crystal Grid Charging: Create a crystal grid using specific crystals aligned with your intention. Arrange them in a geometric pattern and place the crystal you want to charge in the center. The combined energy of the crystals in the grid will charge the central crystal.

- Reiki or Energy Charging: If you are attuned to Reiki or other energy healing modalities, you can channel energy into the crystal by holding it in your hands and visualizing the energy flowing into it. Set the intention that the crystal is being charged with your desired energy.

4. Programming and Setting Intentions: After cleansing and charging, it's essential to program the crystal with your specific intention. Hold the crystal in your hands, focus on your desired outcome, and visualize the energy of your intention flowing into the crystal. State your intention clearly and affirm that the crystal is now aligned with your goal.

5. Regular Maintenance: Crystals may accumulate energies over time, so it's recommended to cleanse and recharge them periodically or after significant use. Trust your intuition to determine when your crystals need cleansing or recharging.

By cleansing and charging your crystals, you ensure they are aligned with your intention and ready to amplify your spellwork. These practices help clear away any unwanted energies and infuse the crystals with focused energy for optimal magical workings. Remember to approach the process with respect, intention, and gratitude for the support the crystals provide in your Wiccan practice.

Chapter 8
Crystal Spellcrafting Basics

1. Setting Intentions: Before beginning any crystal spellwork, clearly define your intention. Be specific and concise about what you want to manifest or achieve through the spell. The intention will guide your choice of crystals and the overall direction of the spell.

2. Choosing Crystals: Select crystals that align with your intention. Refer to their energetic properties and correspondences to find the most suitable ones. Consider color symbolism, elemental associations, chakra correspondences, and the specific qualities of each crystal. Trust your intuition when selecting crystals that resonate with your intention.

3. Cleansing and Charging: Cleanse and charge your chosen crystals using the methods mentioned earlier. Clearing away any previous energies and infusing them with fresh, aligned energy enhances their effectiveness

in the spell.

4. Creating Sacred Space: Set up a dedicated space for your crystal spellwork. Cleanse and consecrate the space to create a sacred and energetically supportive environment. Arrange your crystals and any other ritual tools in a way that feels intuitive and harmonious.

5. Ritual Preparation: Prepare yourself for the spellwork by grounding and centering your energy. You may choose to perform a meditation, engage in deep breathing exercises, or practice visualization techniques. This helps you attune to the energy of the crystals and the spell's intention.

6. Spell Construction: Design the structure and steps of your crystal spell. Consider the specific actions, words, and gestures involved. Incorporate the crystals in a way that enhances the energy and intention of the spell. It could involve arranging the crystals in a specific pattern, holding them in your hands during the spell, or placing them strategically around a candle or other ritual tools.

7. Energizing and Activating the Crystals: As you perform the spell, focus your energy and intention on each crystal. Visualize the energy flowing from your intention into the crystals, activating their metaphysical properties. You may choose to speak affirmations or incanta-

tions, sing chants, or use other ritual elements to charge the crystals further.

8. Time and Duration: Consider the timing and duration of your crystal spell. You may choose to perform the spell during a specific moon phase, planetary alignment, or Sabbat that enhances your intention. Additionally, decide if the spell will be a one-time work or if it requires ongoing attention or repetition.

9. Closing the Spell: Once the spell is complete, express gratitude to the crystals, the divine, and any deities or spirits you invoked during the spell. Close the energy by releasing excess energy or grounding yourself through visualization or other grounding techniques.

10. Post-Spell Care: After the spell, take care of your crystals. Store them in a safe and energetically clean space. You may choose to recharge them periodically or cleanse them if you feel they have absorbed negative energies.

Remember, practice and experience are essential in refining your crystal spell crafting skills. As you gain confidence, feel free to experiment with different crystal combinations, rituals, and techniques. Adapt the basics to suit your personal style and intuition, and trust in the power of crystals to enhance and manifest your intentions in your Wiccan spellwork.

Chapter 9

Setting up a sacred space for crystal magic

CREATING A SACRED SPACE for your crystal magic rituals helps to establish a focused and energetically supportive environment. Here are some steps to guide you in setting up a sacred space:

1. Cleansing the Space: Begin by cleansing the physical space where you plan to conduct your crystal magic. You can do this by smudging with sage, palo santo, or other cleansing herbs, or by using sound vibrations from bells, singing bowls, or rattles. Clearing the space removes any stagnant or negative energies, creating a fresh energetic foundation.

2. Clearing Your Mind: Take a few moments to clear your mind and center yourself. You can do this through deep breathing exercises, meditation, or any other grounding technique that works for you. This allows you to release distractions and align your focus with the intention of

the ritual.

3. Setting an Altar: Create a designated altar space where you will place your crystals, ritual tools, and any other items that are relevant to your practice. This can be a small table, shelf, or any flat surface that you can decorate and dedicate to your magical work.

4. Choosing Meaningful Items: Select items to adorn your altar that hold personal significance or resonate with the energy of your intention. These can include statues or representations of deities, symbols, candles, flowers, feathers, or any other sacred objects that inspire you. Consider incorporating natural elements, such as stones, shells, or plants, to connect with the Earth's energy.

5. Arranging Crystals: Place your chosen crystals on the altar in a way that feels aesthetically pleasing and energetically aligned. You can arrange them based on their properties, colors, or specific intentions. Trust your intuition and create a layout that resonates with you.

6. Ritual Tools: If you have any specific ritual tools, such as an athame (ritual knife), wand, chalice, or divination tools, include them on your altar. These tools can enhance your connection to the ritual and serve as conduits for your energy.

7. Sacred Symbols: Incorporate sacred symbols that hold personal or spiritual significance to you. This can include runes, sigils, pentacles, or any other symbols that represent your intentions or the energies you are working with.

8. Lighting Candles: Light candles on your altar to symbolize the presence of divine energy and to invoke the element of fire. Choose colors that align with your intention or use white candles to represent purity and spirituality.

9. Invocation and Blessing: Take a moment to invoke the divine or any deities, guides, or spirits you work with. Offer a prayer or a blessing, expressing your gratitude for their presence and asking for their guidance and support during your crystal magic rituals.

10. Personalization and Intention: Remember that your sacred space is a reflection of your unique spiritual practice. Feel free to add personal touches, artwork, or other items that inspire and uplift you. Set your intention for the space to be a sacred container for your crystal magic, infused with love, light, and positive energy.

Regularly maintain and refresh your sacred space, keeping it clean, organized, and energetically charged. By creating a dedicated and intentional space for your crystal magic, you establish a sacred connection to the energies you work with, enhancing the effectiveness and potency of your rituals.

Chapter 10

Casting circles and invoking elemental energies

CASTING A CIRCLE IS a common practice in many magical traditions, including Wicca. It creates a sacred and protected space where you can work with the energies of the elements and perform your crystal magic. Here is a guide to casting circles and invoking elemental energies:

1. Preparation: Before casting a circle, gather the tools you will need, such as a wand, athame, or your pointing finger, and any representations of the four elements (earth, air, fire, and water) that resonate with you. You may also want to have candles or objects in the corresponding colors for each element.

2. Centering and Grounding: Take a moment to center yourself and ground your energy. Breathe deeply, focusing on your intention and connecting with the energy of the Earth. Visualize roots growing from your feet into the Earth, anchoring you and stabilizing your energy.

3. Purification: Walk around the perimeter of the circle, either physically or symbolically, using your wand, athame, or pointing finger, to mark the boundary. As you do this, visualize a pure, white light forming a protective barrier around the circle, sealing off any negative or unwanted energies.

4. Invoking the Elements: Begin by invoking the elemental energies at each cardinal direction, starting in the east and moving clockwise (or counterclockwise if it aligns with your tradition). As you face each direction, call upon the corresponding element:

    - East/Air: Visualize or hold an object that represents the element of air, such as a feather or incense. Call upon the energy of the east and say words that invoke the qualities of air, such as communication, intellect, and inspiration.

    - South/Fire: Visualize or hold an object that represents the element of fire, such as a candle or a small flame. Call upon the energy of the south and speak words that invoke the qualities of fire, such as passion, transformation, and creativity.

    - West/Water: Visualize or hold an object that represents the element of water, such as a seashell or a small bowl of water. Call upon the energy of the west and express words that invoke the qualities of water, such as emotions, intuition, and healing.

- North/Earth: Visualize or hold an object that represents the element of earth, such as a crystal or a small dish of soil. Call upon the energy of the north and state words that invoke the qualities of earth, such as stability, abundance, and grounding.

5. Circle Completion: After invoking the elements, return to the east, completing the circle. As you do so, visualize the elemental energies blending together, forming a harmonious and balanced circle of power.

6. Working within the Circle: Once the circle is cast, you can perform your crystal magic, rituals, or spells. The circle acts as a container for focused energy, amplifying your intentions and protecting your space.

7. Closing the Circle: When you have completed your work, it is essential to close the circle to release the energies and to honor the elements. This can be done by retracing your steps counterclockwise or through a specific closing ritual or prayer. Thank the elemental energies for their presence and release them with gratitude.

Remember to adapt the casting of circles and invocation of elemental energies to align with your personal beliefs, traditions, and practices. As you gain experience, you may develop your own variations and rituals that feel most authentic and effective for your crystal magic and Wiccan practice.

Chapter 11

Crafting and consecrating ritual tools for crystal spells

CRAFTING AND CONSECRATING RITUAL tools for your crystal spells adds a personal touch and deepens your connection to your magical practice. Here are some steps to guide you in crafting and consecrating your ritual tools:

1. Determine Your Tools: Identify the ritual tools you would like to create or consecrate for your crystal spells. Common tools include wands, athames (ritual knives), chalices, and bowls. You may also choose to craft or personalize additional tools that are meaningful to you, such as a crystal grid board or a divination tool.

2. Select Materials: Choose materials that resonate with your intentions and the purpose of each tool. For a wand, you may consider using a specific wood that holds energetic properties, such as oak for strength or willow for intuition. If crafting an athame, select a blade material that aligns with your energy, such as stainless

steel or obsidian.

3. Craft with Intention: As you create or modify your ritual tools, infuse them with your intentions. Focus your energy and visualize the purpose of each tool, imbuing it with the specific energies and qualities you desire. Incorporate symbols, carvings, or inscriptions that hold personal meaning or correspond to the tool's purpose.

4. Personalize and Decorate: Add personal touches to your tools to make them uniquely yours. You may choose to paint, carve, or decorate them with symbols, colors, or gemstones that align with your practice. Trust your intuition and let your creativity guide you.

5. Cleansing and Clearing: Before consecrating your tools, cleanse them of any previous energies or vibrations they may have accumulated. This can be done through smudging, bathing them in moonlight or sunlight, or using other methods of energetic cleansing that resonate with you.

6. Consecration Ritual: Perform a consecration ritual to infuse your tools with sacred and empowered energy. Find a quiet and sacred space where you can focus your intention and connect with the divine or your chosen deities.

- Light candles or incense to create a sacred ambiance and set the mood.

- Call upon the divine or specific deities that resonate with your practice. Express your intent to consecrate and bless your tools for the purpose of crystal spells and magic.

- Hold each tool in your hands, close your eyes, and visualize a vibrant, pure light surrounding it. Speak words of dedication and consecration, affirming that the tool is now a sacred instrument of your magical practice.

- Pass the tool through the smoke of incense or over the flame of a candle to cleanse and purify it further, while stating your intention for the tool's purpose.

- Place the tool on your altar or a dedicated space, and allow it to absorb the energy of the ritual. You may leave it on the altar for a specific period or overnight to charge it further with the energy of the sacred space.

7. Regular Care and Maintenance: Treat your ritual tools with respect and care. Clean and cleanse them periodically to keep their energy clear and vibrant. Store them in a safe and sacred space when not in use, and handle

them with reverence and gratitude during your crystal spells and rituals.

Crafting and consecrating your ritual tools for crystal spells is a sacred and personal practice that deepens your connection to your magical work. Allow your creativity to flow, infuse your tools with intention, and honor them as sacred instruments of your Wiccan practice.

Chapter 12

Crystal Spells for Love and Relationships

Love and relationships hold a special place in our lives, and crystal spells can be a powerful tool for attracting love, enhancing existing relationships, and fostering harmony. In this section, we will explore various crystal spells specifically designed to work with matters of the heart.

A. Attracting Love:

1. Rose Quartz Love Spell: Use rose quartz, the stone of love, to attract a new romantic partner into your life. Charge a rose quartz crystal under the light of a full moon and place it on your altar. Light a pink or red candle and visualize the qualities you desire in a partner. Speak affirmations of love and open yourself to receiving love in your life.

2. Love Sachet Spell: Create a love sachet by placing dried rose petals, lavender, and a small rose quartz crystal in a pink or red pouch. Tie it with a ribbon, infusing it

with your intention for love. Carry the sachet with you or place it under your pillow to attract love and romance into your life.

B. Enhancing Existing Relationships:

1. Relationship Healing Crystal Grid: Create a crystal grid using crystals such as amethyst, rose quartz, and clear quartz to heal and strengthen your existing relationship. Place the crystals in a geometric pattern on a cloth or a grid board. Focus your intention on harmonizing and resolving any issues within the relationship. Meditate or perform a ritual within the grid, allowing the crystals to amplify the energy of love and healing.

2. Communication and Harmony Spell: Use blue lace agate and sodalite to enhance communication and harmony in your relationship. Hold the crystals in your hands and visualize clear and loving communication between you and your partner. Speak affirmations of understanding, empathy, and cooperation. Keep the crystals near your bedside or in a common area to promote peaceful and open communication.

C. Self-Love and Empowerment:

1. Self-Love Bath Ritual: Create a nurturing and self-loving ritual by adding rose quartz, amethyst, and dried rose petals to your bathwater. As you soak in the bath, visualize self-love and acceptance permeating your be-

ing. Speak affirmations of self-worth and empowerment. Allow the crystals and the energy of the water to cleanse and rejuvenate your spirit.

2. Confidence Spell: Work with citrine, sunstone, or tiger's eye to boost your confidence and self-esteem. Hold the crystal in your hand and connect with its energy. Visualize yourself radiating confidence and self-assuredness in all areas of your life. Carry the crystal with you or wear it as jewelry as a reminder of your inner strength.

Remember, when working with crystal spells for love and relationships, it is important to align your intentions with the highest good of all involved. Always respect the free will and boundaries of others, and approach these spells with love, integrity, and pure intentions. Trust in the power of crystals and the energy of love to bring about positive transformations in your romantic life.

Chapter 13

Attracting love and enhancing romantic relationships with crystals

CRYSTALS HAVE LONG BEEN associated with love and romance, and they can be used to attract new love into your life or enhance the connection in an existing relationship. Here are some crystal spells and practices to help you in attracting love and deepening your romantic relationships:

1. Rose Quartz Love Spell: Rose quartz is the quintessential crystal for love and is known for its ability to attract and enhance romantic relationships. To perform a rose quartz love spell, place a piece of rose quartz on your heart chakra while visualizing yourself surrounded by love. Speak affirmations that reflect the qualities you seek in a partner or the love you wish to cultivate. Carry the rose quartz with you or place it under your pillow to amplify the energy of love.

2. Love Crystal Grid: Create a crystal grid specifically de-

signed to attract love into your life. Choose crystals associated with love, such as rose quartz, rhodochrosite, and rhodonite. Place them in a geometric pattern on a grid cloth or board. Set your intention for love and visualize yourself in a fulfilling and loving relationship. Keep the crystal grid in a prominent place, and periodically recharge the energy by holding your intention and connecting with the crystals.

3. Aphrodite Ritual: Invoke the energy of Aphrodite, the goddess of love, beauty, and passion, to attract love and enhance your romantic relationships. Create an altar dedicated to Aphrodite and adorn it with symbols and offerings associated with love, such as red or pink candles, rose petals, and rose essential oil. Place crystals like rose quartz and emerald on the altar. Light the candles, focus on the energy of Aphrodite, and ask for her blessings in matters of love. Express your gratitude and leave the altar set up for a period of time as a focal point for love energy.

4. Relationship Communication Spell: Communication is vital in any romantic relationship. Use blue lace agate or sodalite crystals to enhance communication and promote understanding between you and your partner. Hold the crystal in your hand and visualize clear and loving communication. Speak affirmations that affirm

open dialogue and empathy. Keep the crystal near you or give it to your partner as a gift to enhance communication within the relationship.

5. Passion and Intimacy Ritual: Use crystals such as carnelian, garnet, or ruby to ignite passion and deepen intimacy in your relationship. Create a sacred space with soft lighting and soothing music. Place the chosen crystals on your bedside table or in the bedroom. Spend quality time together, engaging in activities that promote connection and intimacy. Allow the energy of the crystals to enhance the passion and deepen the bond between you and your partner.

Remember, crystals are tools that can assist you in your journey of love and relationships. While they can enhance the energy and create a positive atmosphere, they should not replace communication, trust, and mutual respect in a relationship. Use these crystal spells and practices as complementary tools, always respecting the free will and boundaries of yourself and others. Open your heart to love and allow the energy of crystals to support and guide you on your romantic journey.

Chapter 14

Healing and restoring harmony in troubled relationships

WHEN A ROMANTIC RELATIONSHIP faces challenges and disharmony, crystals can be utilized to promote healing, restore balance, and foster renewed love and understanding. Here are some crystal spells and practices to help in healing and restoring harmony in troubled relationships:

1. Amethyst Healing Ritual: Amethyst is a powerful crystal known for its calming and healing properties. Create a peaceful and sacred space for you and your partner. Place amethyst crystals around the space or hold them in your hands. Close your eyes, take deep breaths, and visualize the healing energy surrounding both of you. Express your feelings and concerns honestly, while holding the intention of finding resolution and restoring harmony. Allow the amethyst's energy to bring about emotional healing and open communication.

2. Forgiveness and Release Spell: Holding onto grudges

and past hurts can hinder the healing process in a troubled relationship. Use crystals such as rose quartz and rhodonite to facilitate forgiveness and release negative emotions. Sit in a quiet space with your partner, each holding a crystal in your hands. Visualize the pain and grievances transforming into love and compassion. Speak words of forgiveness, both for yourself and your partner. Release the crystals into a body of water, symbolizing the release of negativity and the beginning of a new chapter of understanding and harmony.

3. Relationship Reconciliation Grid: Create a crystal grid focused on reconciling and restoring harmony in your troubled relationship. Choose crystals like rhodochrosite, green aventurine, and clear quartz. Arrange them in a grid pattern on a cloth or grid board. Visualize the grid drawing in healing energy and transforming the relationship into one of love, understanding, and harmony. Place a photograph of you and your partner in the center of the grid to infuse it with your intentions. Leave the grid in place for as long as needed, periodically recharging it with your focused intention.

4. Harmonizing Couples Bath: Prepare a bath for you and your partner with crystals and herbs that promote love, harmony, and emotional healing. Add rose quartz, clear quartz, and lavender essential oil to the bathwater. Light

candles around the tub and play soft, soothing music. Step into the bath together, holding hands, and allow the warm water and the crystal energy to envelop you. Visualize the negative energies dissolving and being replaced by love, understanding, and harmony. Take this time to reconnect and share your desires for a renewed and harmonious relationship.

5. Couples Meditation with Crystals: Engage in a couple's meditation using crystals to deepen your connection and restore harmony. Sit facing each other, each holding a crystal-like rose quartz or green aventurine. Close your eyes and synchronize your breath. Visualize a golden light surrounding both of you, radiating love and healing energy. Set an intention to listen and understand each other's perspectives without judgment. Speak words of love and appreciation to each other, reaffirming your commitment to working together and restoring harmony in your relationship.

Remember, healing and restoring harmony in a troubled relationship takes time and effort from both partners. Crystals can support and amplify the healing process, but they are not a substitute for open communication, professional guidance if needed, and a willingness to work through challenges together. Approach these crystal spells and practices with patience, love, and a genuine desire for healing and harmony in your relationship.

Chapter 15

Strengthening bonds and promoting self-love using crystal magic

CRYSTAL MAGIC CAN BE a powerful tool for strengthening bonds in relationships and cultivating self-love. Whether you want to deepen the connection with a loved one or enhance your own sense of self-worth, here are some crystal spells and practices to help you in strengthening bonds and promoting self-love:

1. Relationship Bonding Ritual: Choose crystals that promote love, unity, and connection, such as rose quartz, garnet, and pink opal. Sit with your partner in a quiet and comfortable space, each holding a crystal in your hands. Close your eyes and visualize a loving, golden light enveloping both of you. Set the intention to deepen your bond and enhance the love between you. Speak words of love, gratitude, and commitment to each other. Allow the energy of the crystals and your shared intention to strengthen the bond in your relationship.

2. Self-Love Affirmation Ritual: Select crystals that resonate with self-love and empowerment, such as clear quartz, rhodonite, or citrine. Find a peaceful space where you can be alone and undisturbed. Hold the chosen crystal in your hand and close your eyes. Take deep breaths and center yourself. Repeat self-love affirmations, such as "I am worthy of love and happiness," "I embrace my authentic self," or "I love and accept myself unconditionally." Visualize yourself surrounded by a loving, pink light that radiates from the crystal. Feel the energy of self-love filling your being.

3. Mirror Love Spell: Stand in front of a mirror with a rose quartz crystal in your hand. Look into your own eyes and affirm your love for yourself. Speak words of appreciation, acknowledging your unique qualities, strengths, and beauty, both inside and out. Hold the rose quartz against your heart and imagine the loving energy being absorbed into your being. Repeat this practice daily to reinforce self-love and build a positive self-image.

4. Gratitude Crystal Jar: Create a gratitude crystal jar to promote love, appreciation, and positivity in your relationships. Find a small jar or container and fill it with rose quartz chips or small tumbled stones. Write down things you are grateful for in your relationships, both

romantic and non-romantic, on small pieces of paper. Fold each piece of paper and place it in the jar along with the crystals. As you add each piece of paper, visualize the love and gratitude flowing into your relationships. Keep the jar in a visible place as a reminder of the love and appreciation you have in your life.

5. Heart Chakra Meditation: Use heart chakra crystals, such as emerald, green aventurine, or rhodonite, to open and balance your heart chakra, promoting love and compassion for yourself and others. Sit in a comfortable position and hold the crystal over your heart center. Close your eyes and focus on your breath. Visualize a green light radiating from your heart, expanding with each breath. Feel the energy of love, acceptance, and healing flowing through your heart chakra. Send love to yourself and extend it to others, fostering a sense of interconnectedness and compassion.

Remember, strengthening bonds and promoting self-love is an ongoing practice that requires patience, intention, and self-reflection. Crystals can serve as supportive tools, but ultimately, the work comes from within. Be open to the energy of the crystals, trust your intuition, and allow the magic of self-love and strengthened bonds to unfold in your life.

Chapter 16

Crystal Spells for Protection and Cleansing

In Wiccan practice, protection and cleansing are essential for maintaining a harmonious and energetically balanced environment. Crystals can be powerful allies in warding off negative energies, shielding against psychic attacks, and purifying the energetic space. In this section, we will explore crystal spells for protection and cleansing:

A. Protective Crystals and Talismans:

1. Black Tourmaline Shield: Use black tourmaline to create a protective shield around yourself and your space. Hold the crystal in your hand and visualize a powerful, impenetrable barrier forming around you. Set the intention that this shield will block any negative energies or harmful influences. Carry black tourmaline with you or place it near the entrances of your home for ongoing protection.

2. Evil Eye Warding Charm: Create a protective charm

against the evil eye using a combination of crystals such as blue kyanite, black obsidian, and hematite. Assemble the crystals on a string or charm bracelet, focusing on their combined protective energies. Wear the charm as a talisman to ward off negativity and protect against malicious intentions.

B. Home Cleansing and Protection Rituals:
1. Clear Quartz Purification Grid: Create a crystal grid using clear quartz points in each corner of your home. Visualize a pure and cleansing light radiating from each crystal, purifying the space of any negative or stagnant energy. Set the intention for a protected and harmonious environment. Leave the grid in place for as long as needed, periodically recharging the crystals and renewing your intention.

2. Sage and Crystal Smoke Cleansing: Use a combination of white sage and crystals to perform a smoke cleansing ritual for your home. Light the sage bundle and let the smoke waft through each room, visualizing it dispelling negative energies. Follow up by using a crystal such as selenite or black tourmaline to "sweep" the smoke through the space, drawing in positive energy and protection. Be sure to open windows or doors for the smoke to exit, allowing negative energy to be released.

C. Psychic Protection and Empowerment:

1. Amethyst Psychic Shield: Utilize the protective properties of amethyst to create a psychic shield. Hold an amethyst crystal in your hand and visualize a violet light surrounding you, forming a barrier against unwanted energies or psychic attacks. Set the intention that only positive and beneficial energies can penetrate this shield. Keep amethyst nearby when engaging in psychic or spiritual practices.

2. Mirror Spell for Energy Reflection: Place a small, portable mirror and a protective crystal such as black tourmaline or obsidian on your altar or in a sacred space. Visualize the mirror reflecting back any negative energy or harmful intentions directed towards you. Set the intention that the mirror acts as a shield, bouncing negative energy back to its source. Use this spell to protect yourself from psychic attacks or unwanted influences.

Remember to cleanse and recharge your protective crystals regularly to maintain their effectiveness. Trust your intuition when selecting crystals for protection and cleansing, as different stones may resonate with you in unique ways. Combine these crystal spells with your intention, focused visualization, and belief in their power to create a protective and purified energetic space.

Chapter 17

Creating crystal amulets and talismans for personal protection

CRYSTAL AMULETS AND TALISMANS are powerful tools that can be worn or carried to provide personal protection and ward off negative energies. By infusing specific crystals with your intentions and wearing them as a protective charm, you can create a personal shield that accompanies you wherever you go. Here are steps to create crystal amulets and talismans for personal protection:

1. Choose a Protective Crystal: Select a crystal that resonates with personal protection, such as black tourmaline, obsidian, amethyst, or hematite. Research the properties and energies of different crystals to find the one that aligns with your specific needs and intentions.

2. Cleanse and Charge the Crystal: Begin by cleansing the crystal to remove any previous energies it may have absorbed. You can do this by smudging it with sage or palo santo, rinsing it under running water, or burying it in

the earth for a period of time. Once cleansed, charge the crystal by placing it under the light of the full moon or sunlight, or by placing it on a crystal cluster or selenite plate.

3. Set Your Intentions: Hold the crystal in your hands and set your intentions for personal protection. Visualize a shield of light forming around you, deflecting negative energies and creating a safe space. State your intentions clearly and specifically, focusing on the qualities of protection, strength, and warding off harm.

4. Choose a Method for Wearing the Crystal: Decide how you want to wear your crystal amulet or talisman. You can create a pendant by wrapping the crystal in wire or attaching it to a chain or cord. Alternatively, you can carry the crystal in a small pouch or pocket, ensuring it remains close to your body.

5. Create the Amulet or Talisman: If you're creating a pendant, carefully wrap the crystal with wire, ensuring it is secure and won't easily come loose. You can add additional beads or charms that align with your intention for added energy. If you prefer a pouch or pocket amulet, sew or secure the crystal inside a small fabric pouch, adding symbols or protective sigils if desired.

6. Empower the Amulet or Talisman: Once your crystal

amulet or talisman is created, hold it in your hands and visualize it being filled with protective energy. Infuse it with your intentions, love, and gratitude. Speak affirmations or prayers that reflect your desire for personal protection and empowerment.

7. Wear or Carry the Amulet/Talisman: Wear or carry your crystal amulet or talisman regularly, allowing it to act as a constant reminder of your intentions and protection. Trust in its energy and believe that it is working to shield and guide you.

Remember to periodically cleanse and recharge your crystal amulet or talisman to maintain its effectiveness. You can do this by using methods like smudging, sunlight/moonlight exposure, or placing it on a crystal cluster overnight.

Creating a crystal amulet or talisman for personal protection is a deeply personal and empowering process. Trust your intuition and choose crystals that resonate with you. With focused intention and the energy of your chosen crystals, your amulet or talisman will serve as a potent tool for personal protection and energetic shielding.

Chapter 18

Shielding and warding spells with crystals for home and sacred spaces

CREATING A SHIELDED AND protected environment is crucial for maintaining the energetic integrity of your home and sacred spaces. By incorporating crystals into your shielding and warding spells, you can enhance the protective energy and create a sacred sanctuary. Here are some steps to perform shielding and warding spells with crystals for your home and sacred spaces:

1. Select Protective Crystals: Choose crystals known for their protective properties, such as black tourmaline, smoky quartz, black obsidian, or selenite. Each crystal carries unique energies that can aid in shielding and warding off negative influences.

2. Cleanse and Charge the Crystals: Start by cleansing the crystals to remove any previous energies. You can do this by smudging them with sage or palo santo, placing them

under running water, or burying them in the earth. After cleansing, charge the crystals by placing them in sunlight, moonlight, or on a selenite charging plate.

3. Set Your Intentions: Hold the crystals in your hands and set your intentions for shielding and warding your home or sacred space. Visualize a protective barrier forming around the space, repelling negative energies and creating a safe haven. State your intentions clearly, focusing on the qualities of protection, security, and positive energy.

4. Placement of Crystals: Strategically place the crystals in key areas of your home or sacred space to establish a protective grid. You can position them near entrances, windows, or in the corners of rooms. Trust your intuition and place them in locations that feel energetically significant to you.

5. Energize the Crystals: Once the crystals are in place, visualize a powerful and impenetrable shield emanating from them. Envision the crystals absorbing and transmuting any negative energies that come into contact with the space. Feel the energy of protection and safety permeating the area.

6. Affirmations and Incantations: Speak affirmations or incantations that reinforce the protective energy. For

example, you can say, "By the power of these crystals, this space is shielded and protected. Negative energies are repelled, and only love and light may enter." Repeat the affirmations or incantations as many times as you feel necessary to strengthen the protective energy.

7. Recharge and Maintain: Regularly cleanse and recharge the crystals to maintain their effectiveness. You can do this by smudging them, placing them in sunlight or moonlight, or using visualization techniques to clear any accumulated negative energy.

8. Intentional Cleansing Rituals: Enhance the shielding and warding spells with regular cleansing rituals. Use techniques such as smudging, sound cleansing with bells or singing bowls, or sprinkling salt water to purify the space and reinforce the protective energy.

Remember, the power of these spells lies in your intention and belief. Trust the energy of the crystals and your ability to create a shielded and protected space. Combine these crystal spells with other protective practices like creating sacred circles, invoking elemental energies, or working with deities to strengthen the energetic barriers in your home or sacred spaces.

Chapter 19

Clearing negative energies and purifying spaces with crystal grids

CRYSTAL GRIDS ARE POWERFUL tools for clearing negative energies and purifying spaces. By arranging crystals in specific geometric patterns and activating them with intention, you can create a focused and amplified energy field that clears and transmutes negative energies. Here's how to use crystal grids to clear negative energies and purify spaces:

1. Select Purifying Crystals: Choose crystals that are known for their purifying and cleansing properties, such as clear quartz, selenite, amethyst, black tourmaline, or citrine. Each crystal carries unique energies that aid in clearing and transmuting negative energies.

2. Choose a Sacred Space: Select a clean and quiet area where you can set up your crystal grid. This can be a table, altar, or any space that feels sacred to you. Ensure that the space is free from clutter and distractions.

3. Cleanse and Charge the Crystals: Begin by cleansing the crystals to remove any previous energies. You can do this by smudging them with sage or palo santo, placing them under running water, or using sound vibrations. Next, charge the crystals with your intention by holding them in your hands and visualizing them being filled with pure and cleansing energy.

4. Set Your Intention: Before arranging the crystals, set your intention for clearing and purifying the space. Visualize the space being bathed in a cleansing light, free from any negative energies or stagnant vibrations. State your intention clearly, focusing on the qualities of purity, clarity, and positive energy.

5. Choose a Crystal Grid Pattern: Select a crystal grid pattern that resonates with your intention. Common grid patterns include the Flower of Life, Seed of Life, or simple geometric shapes like a circle or square. You can find pre-made crystal grid cloths or templates, or create your own by drawing the pattern on a piece of paper.

6. Arrange the Crystals: Place the crystals on the grid pattern, following your intuition or a specific crystal placement guide. Start with a central crystal, which acts as the anchor or generator. Surround it with additional crystals, creating a symmetrical or balanced arrangement. You can also incorporate other elements, such as flow-

ers, herbs, or sacred symbols, to enhance the grid.

7. Activate the Grid: Once the crystals are arranged, activate the grid by channeling your intention and energy into it. You can do this by placing your hands over the crystals and visualizing a beam of light connecting all the crystals, forming a powerful energetic network. State affirmations or prayers that reinforce your intention for clearing and purifying the space.

8. Maintenance and Cleansing: Leave the crystal grid in place for as long as you feel necessary to clear and purify the space. Periodically cleanse and recharge the crystals to maintain their effectiveness. You can do this by smudging the grid, placing it in sunlight or moonlight, or using sound vibrations.

Remember, the crystal grid is a tool that amplifies your intention and energy. Trust in the power of the crystals and your ability to create a purified space. Combine crystal grids with other purification practices like smudging, sound cleansing, or intentional rituals to enhance the clearing process.

Chapter 20

Crystal Spells for Healing and Well-being

CRYSTALS HAVE LONG BEEN used for their healing properties, promoting balance, and enhancing overall well-being. In this section, we will explore various crystal spells for healing and nurturing your mind, body, and spirit:

A. Crystal Healing Grid for Self-Care:

1. Select Healing Crystals: Choose a selection of crystals known for their healing properties, such as amethyst, rose quartz, clear quartz, citrine, or green aventurine. Each crystal carries unique energies that support different aspects of healing and well-being.

2. Create a Sacred Space: Find a quiet and peaceful area where you can set up a crystal healing grid. Clear the space of any clutter and create a serene ambiance by lighting candles, playing soft music, or using essential oils.

3. Cleanse and Charge the Crystals: Begin by cleansing the crystals to remove any stagnant or negative energies they may have absorbed. Use your preferred method, such as smudging, sound cleansing, or running water. Then, charge the crystals with your intention by holding them in your hands and envisioning them being filled with healing and nurturing energy.

4. Set Your Healing Intention: Before arranging the crystals, set your intention for healing and well-being. Focus on the areas of your life or specific health concerns you wish to address. State your intention clearly, focusing on positive affirmations and the desired outcome of your healing journey.

5. Create the Crystal Healing Grid: Arrange the crystals in a pattern that feels intuitively right to you. You can use a geometric pattern, such as a circle or flower of life, or create your own design. Place a larger crystal, such as a clear quartz point, in the center as the focal point.

6. Activate the Healing Grid: Activate the crystal healing grid by visualizing a beam of healing light connecting all the crystals. See this light expanding and filling the space with healing energy. Spend a few moments connecting with the grid and setting your intentions for healing and well-being.

7. Receiving the Healing Energy: Sit or lie down near the crystal healing grid, allowing yourself to relax and be receptive to the healing energy. Visualize the healing light from the crystals flowing into your body, soothing and nourishing every cell. Breathe deeply and allow yourself to fully receive the healing energy.

B. Crystal Elixir for Physical Healing:
1. Choose a Healing Crystal: Select a crystal that aligns with the specific physical healing you seek. For example, amethyst for soothing headaches, citrine for boosting energy, or rose quartz for promoting self-healing and love.

2. Prepare the Crystal Elixir: Cleanse the chosen crystal and place it in a glass or jar filled with filtered water. Set the container in a place where it can be exposed to sunlight or moonlight for several hours. This will infuse the water with the crystal's healing energy.

3. Charge the Elixir with Intentions: While the crystal is infusing the water, hold the container in your hands and set your healing intentions. Visualize the water being filled with the healing energy of the crystal and the desired outcome of your physical healing. State affirmations or prayers that support your intentions.

4. Drink the Crystal Elixir: Once the water is infused with

the crystal's energy, strain the water to remove the crystal and drink the elixir. As you consume the elixir, imagine the healing energy entering your body, supporting your physical well-being, and promoting the desired healing outcome.

C. Crystal Meditation for Emotional Healing:
1. Select an Emotional Healing Crystal: Choose a crystal known for its emotional healing properties, such as amethyst, rose quartz, labradorite, or blue lace agate. These crystals can assist in releasing emotional blockages, soothing anxiety, and promoting inner peace.

2. Create a Sacred Space: Find a quiet and comfortable space where you can sit undisturbed for your crystal meditation. Arrange candles, cushions, or any other items that create a serene and calming atmosphere.

3. Hold the Healing Crystal: Hold the chosen crystal in your hand or place it on your heart center. Close your eyes and take several deep breaths to center yourself.

4. Set Your Intention: Set your intention for emotional healing and release. Focus on any specific emotions or patterns you wish to address. State your intention clearly, emphasizing self-compassion and a desire for emotional well-being.

5. Visualize the Healing Energy: With the crystal in hand, visualize a gentle and soothing light emanating from the crystal, enveloping your entire body. Feel this light penetrating any emotional wounds or areas of tension, gradually releasing and healing them.

6. Embrace the Healing Process: Allow yourself to fully experience and embrace any emotions that arise during the meditation. Trust that the crystal's energy is supporting you in this healing journey. Release any emotional baggage that no longer serves you, and invite in feelings of love, peace, and emotional balance.

7. Express Gratitude: Once the meditation is complete, express gratitude to the crystal for its healing energy and the emotional healing you have experienced. Take a moment to journal or reflect on any insights or shifts that occurred during the meditation.

Remember, crystal spells for healing and well-being should be used as a complementary practice to conventional medical or therapeutic approaches. Always seek professional advice for any health concerns. Crystals can support and enhance your healing journey, but they should not replace professional medical care.

Chapter 21

Utilizing crystals for physical healing and pain relief

CRYSTALS HAVE BEEN USED for centuries to aid in physical healing and pain relief. Their unique energetic properties can support the body's natural healing processes and help alleviate discomfort. Here are some ways to utilize crystals for physical healing and pain relief:

1. Crystal Placement: Choose crystals that are known for their healing properties, such as amethyst, clear quartz, citrine, or hematite. Place the crystals directly on or near the affected area to promote healing and pain relief. For example, you can place amethyst on your forehead for headache relief or hold hematite near a sore joint or muscle.

2. Crystal Massage: Use smooth, polished crystals like rose quartz, green aventurine, or selenite to perform a crystal massage. Gently rub the crystal over the affected area in circular motions, allowing its energy to penetrate the

tissues and promote healing. Combine this technique with a carrier oil or lotion for added relaxation and comfort.

3. Crystal Elixirs: Create a crystal elixir by placing a cleansed crystal in a glass or jar of filtered water. Allow the water to absorb the crystal's energy for a few hours, then drink the infused water. This can help promote overall well-being and assist in the body's healing process.

4. Crystal Grids: Set up a crystal grid specifically designed for physical healing and pain relief. Choose crystals that resonate with your intention, such as malachite, turquoise, or amber. Arrange them in a grid pattern and activate the grid by connecting the crystals with your intention for healing. Place the grid near you or on the affected area to benefit from the combined energy of the crystals.

5. Crystal Energy Healing: Seek the assistance of a trained crystal healer or energy practitioner who can use specific crystals and techniques to target your physical ailments. They may place crystals on your body's energy centers or use specialized layouts to promote healing and pain relief.

6. Meditation with Crystals: Incorporate crystals into

your meditation practice to enhance relaxation, promote healing, and alleviate pain. Hold a crystal in your hand or place it on your body while meditating, focusing your attention on the crystal's energy and allowing it to support your physical well-being.

Remember to combine crystal healing practices with any necessary medical treatments and consult a healthcare professional for severe or chronic conditions. Crystals can provide complementary support to your overall well-being, but they are not a substitute for professional medical care. Trust your intuition when selecting crystals and experiment with different techniques to find what works best for you.

Chapter 22

Enhancing emotional well-being and releasing negative patterns

CRYSTALS CAN BE POWERFUL allies in promoting emotional well-being and supporting the release of negative patterns or emotions. Their energetic vibrations can help balance emotions, bring clarity, and facilitate healing on an emotional level. Here are some ways to utilize crystals for enhancing emotional well-being and releasing negative patterns:

1. Crystal Meditation: Choose a crystal that resonates with the specific emotional qualities you wish to enhance or release, such as rose quartz for self-love, amethyst for calming the mind, or citrine for uplifting energy. Hold the crystal in your hand or place it on your heart center during meditation. Focus your attention on the crystal's energy and allow it to assist in shifting your emotional state and releasing negative patterns.

2. Crystal Affirmations: Select a crystal that aligns with your desired emotional state or intention, such as blue

lace agate for soothing communication or black tourmaline for grounding and protection. Hold the crystal in your hand and state affirmations that support your emotional well-being. For example, "I release all negative patterns and embrace emotional healing and positivity."

3. Crystal Elixirs or Gem Water: Create a crystal elixir or gem water by placing cleansed crystals in a glass or jar of filtered water. Allow the water to absorb the crystal's energy for several hours or overnight. Drink the infused water to enhance your emotional well-being and support the release of negative patterns or emotions. Remember to use safe crystals for creating gem water, as some crystals may contain toxic elements.

4. Crystal Journaling: Use crystals during your journaling practice to explore and release negative patterns or emotions. Hold a crystal in your hand while writing and allow its energy to guide your reflections. Write about any negative patterns or emotions you wish to release, expressing your intentions for healing and transformation.

5. Crystal Grids for Emotional Healing: Create a crystal grid specifically designed for emotional healing and releasing negative patterns. Choose crystals that resonate with emotional balance and healing, such as moonstone, labradorite, or rhodonite. Arrange the crystals in

a pattern that feels intuitive to you and set your intention for emotional healing and releasing negative patterns. Activate the grid by connecting the crystals and visualize the release of negative patterns while inviting in positive emotions and healing.

6. Crystal Bath or Shower: Incorporate crystals into your bath or shower routine to cleanse and uplift your emotions. Place cleansed crystals near your bathtub or in a pouch that hangs from the showerhead. Allow the water to flow over the crystals, infusing it with their energy. Visualize the water washing away any negative emotions or patterns, leaving you feeling refreshed and emotionally balanced.

Remember to cleanse and recharge your crystals regularly to maintain their energetic potency. Trust your intuition when selecting crystals for emotional well-being and releasing negative patterns. Crystals can provide gentle support on your emotional journey, but they are not a substitute for professional therapy or medical advice. Seek professional help if you are experiencing severe emotional distress or mental health concerns.

Chapter 23

Promoting spiritual growth and connecting with higher consciousness using crystals

CRYSTALS CAN BE POWERFUL tools for promoting spiritual growth and deepening your connection with higher consciousness. Their unique energetic properties can assist in opening channels of spiritual awareness, amplifying intuition, and facilitating profound spiritual experiences. Here are some ways to utilize crystals for promoting spiritual growth and connecting with higher consciousness:

1. Crystal Meditation: Choose a crystal that resonates with your spiritual intentions, such as clear quartz, amethyst, selenite, or moldavite. Find a quiet and comfortable space where you can sit undisturbed. Hold the crystal in your hand or place it in front of you. Close your eyes, take several deep breaths, and allow yourself to relax. Focus your attention on the crystal's energy and allow it to guide you into a deep meditative state. Use this time to connect with your inner self, explore higher

realms of consciousness, and receive spiritual insights and guidance.

2. Crystal Grid for Spiritual Alignment: Create a crystal grid specifically designed to promote spiritual alignment and connection. Choose crystals that resonate with spiritual growth and higher consciousness, such as clear quartz points, amethyst clusters, or labradorite. Set your intention for spiritual expansion and place the crystals in a sacred geometric pattern. Activate the grid by connecting the crystals and visualize yourself being aligned with higher frequencies of energy and consciousness.

3. Crystal Scrying: Use crystals for scrying, a technique that involves gazing into a crystal's reflective or translucent surface to receive spiritual insights. Choose a crystal with a flat surface or one that naturally forms a window or inclusion. Cleanse and charge the crystal, then hold it in your hand or place it on a table in front of you. Relax your gaze and allow your mind to quiet. Focus on the crystal's surface, allowing images, symbols, or messages to come forward. Trust your intuition and interpret the information received as guidance for your spiritual growth.

4. Crystal Pendulum: Work with a crystal pendulum to enhance your intuitive abilities and receive spiritual

guidance. Choose a crystal pendulum that resonates with you, such as amethyst, clear quartz, or lapis lazuli. Cleanse and charge the pendulum, then hold it between your thumb and forefinger. Establish a clear communication protocol with the pendulum, such as assigning specific movements to indicate "yes," "no," or "undecided." Ask spiritual questions and observe the pendulum's movements for guidance and insight.

5. Crystal Dreamwork: Place a cleansed crystal, such as amethyst or clear quartz, under your pillow or on your bedside table before going to sleep. This can enhance dream recall, promote lucid dreaming, and facilitate spiritual experiences during sleep. Keep a dream journal nearby to record your dreams and any spiritual insights or messages received. Reflect on your dreams for spiritual growth and understanding.

6. Crystal Rituals and Ceremonies: Incorporate crystals into your spiritual rituals and ceremonies to amplify their energy and intention. Use specific crystals that align with the purpose of your ritual, such as rose quartz for love and compassion or citrine for abundance and manifestation. Place crystals on your altar, wear them as jewelry or hold them in your hand during the ritual. Allow the crystals to energetically support your spiritual intentions and enhance the sacredness of the ceremony.

Remember to cleanse and recharge your crystals regularly, as they can absorb energies from their environment and previous uses. Trust your intuition when working with crystals for spiritual growth, and be open to the experiences and insights that come forward. Crystals can serve as powerful catalysts for spiritual transformation, but they are not a substitute for personal growth, self-reflection, or spiritual practice.

Chapter 24

Crystal Spells for Abundance and Prosperity

CRYSTALS HAVE LONG BEEN used as tools for attracting abundance and prosperity into one's life. Their unique energetic properties can assist in shifting one's mindset, removing blockages, and aligning with the energy of abundance. Here are some crystal spells and techniques to manifest wealth and financial success:

1. Crystal Abundance Grid: Create an abundance crystal grid by selecting crystals known for their prosperity properties, such as citrine, green aventurine, pyrite, or tiger's eye. Place a larger crystal, such as a citrine cluster, in the center of the grid as the focal point. Surround it with smaller crystals of your choice, creating a geometric pattern. As you set up the grid, visualize your intentions for abundance and financial success. Activate the grid by connecting the crystals' energies and repeating affirmations of prosperity.

2. Wealth Attraction Crystal Jar: Find a small glass jar or container and fill it with a mixture of prosperity crystals, such as citrine, pyrite, green jade, and aventurine. Hold the jar in your hands and infuse it with your intentions for wealth and financial abundance. Place the jar in a prominent location in your home or on your desk, allowing the crystals' energy to radiate and attract abundance into your life.

3. Money Manifestation Ritual: Gather a green candle, a piece of paper, a pen, and a prosperity crystal like citrine or green aventurine. Light the candle and sit in a quiet space. On the paper, write down your financial goals and intentions, being specific and positive. Hold the prosperity crystal in your hand and visualize yourself already living in abundance. Feel the excitement and gratitude for the wealth that is flowing into your life. Burn the paper in the candle flame, releasing your intentions to the universe. Place the crystal near the candle as a reminder of your prosperity intentions.

4. Crystal Visualization Meditation: Find a comfortable and quiet space where you won't be disturbed. Hold a prosperity crystal of your choice, such as citrine, in your hand or place it in front of you. Close your eyes and take several deep breaths to relax. Visualize yourself surrounded by golden light, symbolizing abundance and

prosperity. See yourself living a life of financial freedom, enjoying the luxuries and opportunities that abundance brings. Allow the crystal's energy to support and amplify your visualization, infusing it with powerful intention and manifesting energy.

5. Abundance Affirmation Ritual: Select a prosperity crystal, such as pyrite or green jade, and hold it in your hand. Repeat affirmations of abundance and prosperity, such as "I am a magnet for wealth and financial success," or "Money flows to me effortlessly and abundantly." Say these affirmations with conviction and belief, allowing the crystal's energy to amplify its vibration. Repeat these affirmations daily, preferably in the morning or before engaging in financial activities.

Remember that while crystals can assist in attracting abundance, it is essential to take inspired action and make wise financial decisions. Crystals work in synergy with your intentions and efforts, serving as supportive tools in your journey toward prosperity and financial success. Stay open to opportunities and trust in the process of manifestation.

Chapter 25

Manifesting abundance and attracting financial prosperity with crystals

CRYSTALS CAN BE POWERFUL allies in manifesting abundance and attracting financial prosperity into your life. Their energetic properties can help shift your mindset, remove blockages, and align your vibration with the energy of abundance. Here are some crystal spells and techniques to manifest abundance and attract financial prosperity:

1. Citrine Abundance Ritual: Citrine is a well-known crystal for attracting wealth and abundance. Create a sacred space for your ritual by clearing and cleansing the energy around you. Hold a citrine crystal in your hands and set your intention for manifesting abundance and financial prosperity. Visualize yourself already in possession of the abundance you desire, feeling the joy and gratitude that comes with it. Place the citrine crystal in a prominent location, such as your wallet or a prosperity corner in your home, as a reminder of your intention.

2. Pyrite Manifestation Spell: Pyrite is often referred to as "Fool's Gold" and is believed to attract wealth and success. Find a pyrite crystal and cleanse it with running water or by smudging it with sage. Hold the pyrite in your hand and visualize your financial goals with clarity and excitement. Speak your intentions out loud, stating your desire for financial prosperity and abundance. Keep the pyrite crystal in your workspace or carry it with you to enhance your manifestation efforts.

3. Green Aventurine Wealth Grid: Green aventurine is a crystal known for its luck and prosperity properties. Create a wealth grid by placing a green aventurine crystal at the center and surrounding it with other crystals associated with abundances, such as citrine, jade, or tiger's eye. As you set up the grid, state your intentions for financial prosperity and visualize the energy of abundance radiating from the crystals. Activate the grid by drawing an invisible line connecting the crystals, forming a cohesive energy field.

4. Prosperity Crystal Elixir: Create a crystal elixir infused with the energy of abundance. Choose crystals like citrine, green aventurine, or jade, and cleanse them thoroughly. Place the cleansed crystals in a glass jar filled with filtered water and let it sit in a sunny spot for a few hours. As the crystals infuse the water with their

energy, it becomes charged with abundance vibrations. Drink the crystal elixir daily, preferably in the morning, to align your energy with financial prosperity.

5. Manifestation Visualization Meditation: Find a quiet and comfortable space where you can relax without any distractions. Hold a crystal that resonates with abundances, such as citrine or green aventurine, in your hand. Close your eyes and take several deep breaths to center yourself. Visualize yourself surrounded by a golden light of abundance, feeling the emotions of financial prosperity. See yourself effortlessly attracting wealth, opportunities, and success. Allow the crystal's energy to amplify your visualization and infuse it with powerful intention.

Remember to trust in the process of manifestation and take inspired action toward your financial goals. Crystals are supportive tools, but they work in synergy with your intentions, mindset, and actions. Stay open to opportunities, practice gratitude for the abundance already present in your life, and allow the energy of crystals to guide and support you on your path to financial prosperity.

Chapter 26

Using crystals for career success and manifestation of goals

CRYSTALS CAN BE VALUABLE allies in manifesting career success and helping you achieve your professional goals. Their energetic properties can enhance focus, boost confidence, attract opportunities, and support your overall career journey. Here are some crystal spells and techniques to harness the power of crystals for career success and goal manifestation:

1. Clear Quartz Clarity Ritual: Clear quartz is a versatile crystal known for its amplifying properties. Begin by cleansing and charging a clear quartz crystal, either by running it under cool water or placing it in sunlight or moonlight. Hold the clear quartz in your hand and set your intention for career success and clarity. Visualize yourself thriving in your desired career, accomplishing your goals, and experiencing fulfillment. Keep the clear quartz crystal on your desk or carry it with you as a reminder of your intentions and to amplify your focus and clarity.

2. Carnelian Confidence Spell: Carnelian is a crystal associated with courage, motivation, and self-confidence. Select a polished carnelian stone and cleanse it thoroughly. Hold the carnelian in your hand and connect with its vibrant energy. Close your eyes and visualize yourself confidently excelling in your career. Feel the sense of empowerment and self-assurance flowing through you. Carry the carnelian with you or place it on your desk to boost your confidence and inspire success in your professional endeavors.

3. Citrine Abundance Ritual for Career Success: Citrine is widely recognized as a crystal of abundance and success. Create a sacred space for your ritual by clearing the energy around you. Hold a citrine crystal in your hand and set your intention for career success and abundance. Visualize yourself achieving your career goals, feeling joyful and fulfilled in your chosen path. Place the citrine crystal on your desk or in your workspace, allowing its energy to infuse your professional endeavors with positivity and success.

4. Green Aventurine Networking Spell: Green aventurine is a crystal associated with luck, opportunity, and networking. Find a green aventurine stone and cleanse it with intention. Hold the green aventurine in your hand and visualize yourself confidently networking, making

connections, and expanding your professional network. Feel the energy of opportunity and abundance flowing through you. Carry the green aventurine with you when attending networking events or important meetings to attract beneficial connections and opportunities.

5. Labradorite Visualization Meditation: Labradorite is a crystal that enhances intuition, inspiration, and creativity. Find a labradorite crystal and cleanse it gently. Sit in a comfortable position and hold the labradorite in your hand. Close your eyes and take several deep breaths to relax. Visualize yourself in your dream career, fully engaged, and inspired by your work. Feel the excitement and passion as you tap into your creative potential. Allow the labradorite's energy to activate your intuition and guide you in making career choices aligned with your highest path.

Remember to set clear intentions, visualize your goals with passion and detail, and trust in the process of manifestation. Crystals can serve as powerful tools, but it is important to take action and make proactive choices to support your career success. Use the energy of crystals as a catalyst and reminder of your intentions, allowing them to amplify your focus, confidence, and alignment with your professional goals.

Chapter 27

Cultivating gratitude and abundance mindset through crystal magic

GRATITUDE AND AN ABUNDANCE mindset are essential for attracting and manifesting more abundance in your life. Crystals can be wonderful allies in cultivating these qualities and shifting your perspective towards gratitude and abundance. Here are some crystal spells and techniques to help you cultivate gratitude and an abundance mindset:

1. Golden Citrine Gratitude Ritual: Citrine is a crystal known for its association with abundance and joy. Find a golden citrine crystal and cleanse it with your intention. Hold the citrine in your hand and reflect on the things you are grateful for in your life. Express gratitude for both big and small blessings. As you hold the crystal, allow its vibrant energy to amplify your feelings of gratitude. Keep the citrine in a gratitude altar or carry it with you as a reminder to focus on gratitude throughout the day.

2. Green Jade Abundance Affirmations: Green jade is a crystal that symbolizes luck, abundance, and prosperity. Find a green jade stone and cleanse it thoroughly. Hold the jade in your hand and repeat affirmations of abundance and gratitude. For example, say, "I am grateful for the abundance that flows into my life. I attract prosperity in all areas." Repeat these affirmations with conviction and allow the jade's energy to amplify their vibration. Carry the green jade with you or place it in your workspace to remind yourself of your abundant mindset.

3. Pyrite Prosperity Meditation: Pyrite, also known as "Fool's Gold," is a crystal associated with wealth, abundance, and manifestation. Find a pyrite crystal and cleanse it with intention. Sit in a quiet space and hold the pyrite in your hand. Close your eyes and take deep breaths to relax. Visualize yourself surrounded by a golden light of abundance and feel gratitude for the abundance already present in your life. Allow the pyrite's energy to enhance your visualization and amplify your feelings of gratitude and abundance.

4. Amethyst Gratitude Journaling: Amethyst is a crystal known for its calming and spiritual properties. Find an amethyst crystal and cleanse it gently. Set up a sacred space for journaling, with the amethyst nearby. Take a

few moments to ground yourself and connect with the crystal's energy. Begin writing in your gratitude journal, listing at least three things you are grateful for each day. As you write, hold the amethyst in your hand or place it on the journal to infuse your gratitude with its calming and spiritual energy.

5. Rose Quartz Self-Love and Gratitude Ritual: Rose quartz is a crystal associated with love, compassion, and self-care. Find a rose quartz crystal and cleanse it with your intention. Sit in a quiet space and hold the rose quartz in your hand. Close your eyes and take deep breaths to center yourself. Reflect on the things you appreciate about yourself and the qualities you love. Feel the love and gratitude for yourself growing with each breath. Place the rose quartz on your heart chakra or carry it with you as a reminder to practice self-love and gratitude.

Remember that cultivating gratitude and an abundance mindset is a daily practice. Incorporating crystals into your rituals and daily life can support and amplify this practice. As you work with crystals, stay open and receptive to the blessings and abundance that surround you, and allow the energy of gratitude to attract even more abundance into your life.

Chapter 28

Crystal Spells for Divination and Intuition

CRYSTALS CAN SERVE AS powerful tools for enhancing divination practices, allowing you to tap into your intuition and receive guidance from higher realms. Here are some crystal spells and techniques to enhance your divination abilities:

1. Amethyst Pendulum Communication: Amethyst is a crystal known for its spiritual properties and connection to higher realms. Find an amethyst pendulum and cleanse it with your intention. Sit in a quiet space and hold the amethyst pendulum by its chain or cord. Set your intention to receive clear and accurate guidance. Begin asking your questions, allowing the pendulum to swing or move in response. The amethyst's energy can help amplify your intuitive connection and provide insightful answers.

2. Labradorite Scrying Ritual: Labradorite is a crystal associated with intuition, psychic abilities, and enhanc-

ing spiritual connections. Find a labradorite stone and cleanse it gently. Set up a sacred space for scrying, with the labradorite placed on a dark cloth or a stand. Dim the lights and relax your mind. Gaze into the labradorite's mesmerizing colors and patterns, allowing your mind to enter a meditative state. Be open to receiving symbols, images, or messages that may arise, trusting in your intuitive interpretation.

3. Clear Quartz Crystal Grid for Tarot Readings: Clear quartz is a versatile crystal known for its amplifying properties. Create a crystal grid for tarot readings by placing clear quartz crystals at the four corners of your tarot spread. The clear quartz amplifies the energy and intention of your tarot reading, enhancing your connection to the cards and allowing for clearer insights. Set your intention for accurate and insightful readings as you lay out the cards.

B. Activating Intuition with Crystal Spells

Crystals can help activate and enhance your intuition, allowing you to access deeper insights and trust your inner guidance. Here are some crystal spells and techniques to activate your intuition:

1. Sodalite Third Eye Activation: Sodalite is a crystal known for its connection to the third eye chakra, intuition, and psychic abilities. Find a sodalite stone and

cleanse it with your intention. Sit in a comfortable position and hold the sodalite in your hand. Close your eyes and take deep breaths to relax. Visualize a vibrant indigo light surrounding your forehead, representing the activation of your third eye. Allow the sodalite's energy to assist in opening and activating your intuition.

2. Lapis Lazuli Meditation for Intuitive Insights: Lapis lazuli is a crystal associated with spiritual growth, intuition, and inner vision. Find a lapis lazuli stone and cleanse it gently. Sit in a quiet space and hold the lapis lazuli in your hand. Close your eyes and focus on your breath, allowing your mind to become still. Visualize a gentle stream of indigo light flowing into your mind, expanding your awareness and intuition. Feel the lapis lazuli's energy supporting you in accessing intuitive insights and wisdom.

3. Moonstone Dream Enhancer: Moonstone is a crystal that enhances intuition, psychic abilities, and dreamwork. Find a moonstone crystal and cleanse it with your intention. Place the moonstone under your pillow before you sleep, setting the intention to enhance your intuitive insights and receive guidance through your dreams. Keep a dream journal nearby to record any significant dreams or intuitive messages you receive upon waking.

Remember, the power of divination and intuition comes from within you. Crystals are tools that can assist and amplify your natural abilities. Trust your intuition, allow yourself to be open and receptive to the guidance received, and use crystals as supportive allies on your divination and intuitive journey.

Chapter 29

Strengthening psychic abilities and intuition with crystal rituals

CRYSTALS CAN BE POWERFUL allies in strengthening your psychic abilities and enhancing your intuition. By incorporating crystal rituals into your practice, you can create a sacred space for deepening your psychic connection and expanding your intuitive gifts. Here are some crystal spells and techniques to strengthen your psychic abilities and intuition:

1. Crystal Charging and Activation: Begin by selecting crystals that resonate with psychic abilities and intuition, such as amethyst, labradorite, clear quartz, or selenite. Cleanse the crystals using your preferred method, such as smudging with sage or placing them under the moonlight. Hold each crystal in your hand and set your intention to amplify your psychic abilities and enhance your intuition. Visualize the crystals being infused with pure, radiant energy. You can then place the crystals on your altar or carry them with you to enhance your intuitive connection throughout the day.

2. Intuitive Crystal Meditation: Find a quiet and comfortable space where you can relax and focus on your breath. Hold a crystal that resonates with your intuition, such as amethyst or lapis lazuli, in your hand. Close your eyes and take several deep breaths, allowing your body and mind to relax. As you breathe, visualize the crystal's energy flowing into your body, filling you with a sense of calmness and inner knowing. Focus your attention on your third eye, the center of intuition, and imagine it opening and expanding. Allow any intuitive insights or messages to come forward without judgment or expectation.

3. Crystal Grid for Psychic Enhancement: Create a crystal grid to amplify and focus your psychic abilities. Select crystals that resonate with psychic gifts, such as amethyst, clear quartz, black obsidian, and fluorite. Place a larger crystal, like amethyst or clear quartz point, in the center as the focal point. Surround it with smaller crystals, creating a geometric pattern. As you place each crystal, state your intention for enhancing your psychic abilities and intuition. Activate the grid by drawing an imaginary line connecting each crystal, infusing it with your intention. Sit or meditate near the crystal grid to tap into its energy and strengthen your psychic connection.

4. Crystal Scrying Ritual: Scrying is a practice that involves gazing into a reflective surface or crystal to receive intuitive insights. Find a crystal ball, black obsidian mirror, or any reflective surface that resonates with you. Cleanse and consecrate the scrying tool using your preferred method. Sit in a dimly lit room and hold the scrying tool in your hands. Allow your mind to relax and focus on the surface of the crystal. Gaze into it, allowing your vision to soften and your intuition to guide you. Be open to receiving symbols, images, or messages that may come forward. Practice regularly to strengthen your scrying abilities and deepen your intuitive connection.

5. Crystal-enhanced Divination Tools: Incorporate crystals into your divination practices to enhance your intuitive abilities. For example, you can place a crystal, such as amethyst or clear quartz, on top of your tarot deck or pendulum to infuse it with additional energy and guidance. Alternatively, you can hold a crystal in your hand while performing a divination reading, allowing its energy to connect you with your intuition and provide deeper insights.

Remember that developing psychic abilities and enhancing intuition is a journey that requires patience, practice, and trust. Crystals can assist in amplifying your inherent gifts, but ultimately, it is your own intuitive connection that drives the process. Stay attuned to your inner guidance, practice regularly, and allow the energy of crystals to support and empower your psychic journey.

Chapter 30

Crystal scrying and crystal pendulum for divination purposes

CRYSTAL SCRYING AND CRYSTAL pendulum are two popular methods of divination that utilize the power of crystals to receive intuitive insights and guidance. Here's how you can effectively use crystal scrying and crystal pendulum for divination purposes:

1. Crystal Scrying:

- Choose a crystal ball, black obsidian mirror, or any reflective crystal surface that resonates with you. Cleanse and consecrate the crystal scrying tool to align it with your intention.

- Find a quiet and dimly lit space where you can comfortably sit and focus without distractions.

- Hold the crystal scrying tool in your hands and take a few deep breaths to relax and center yourself.

- Gaze into the surface of the crystal without focusing on any particular point. Allow your vision to soften and become receptive.

- Be open to receiving symbols, images, or impressions that come to your awareness. Trust your intuition and allow the messages to unfold naturally.

- You can ask specific questions or simply remain open to general guidance. Remember that scrying is a practice of allowing insights to emerge rather than seeking direct answers.

- Take note of the symbols, images, or messages you receive during the scrying session. Trust your intuitive interpretation and reflect on their meaning in relation to your questions or concerns.

2. Crystal Pendulum:

- Choose a crystal pendulum that resonates with your intuition and intention. Clear quartz, amethyst, or any other crystal that aligns with divination and intuition can be used.

- Cleanse and consecrate the crystal pendulum to clear any residual energies and program it with your intention for divination.

- Find a quiet and comfortable space where you can sit and hold the pendulum without interruptions.

- Hold the pendulum by its chain, allowing it to hang freely. Ensure that your hand is steady and relaxed.

- Establish a clear signal for "yes" and "no" responses by asking the pendulum to show you each response. Observe the direction in which the pendulum swings or rotates for each answer.

- Begin by asking simple and clear questions, focusing on one question at a time. Allow the pendulum to move and respond, indicating the answer through its motion.

- Trust your intuition and the signals from the pendulum. Take note of the answers and use your discernment in interpreting them.

- Remember that practice and experience will strengthen your connection with the pendulum and enhance the accuracy of your divination readings.

In both crystal scrying and crystal pendulum practices, it is important to approach them with an open and receptive mindset. Trust your intuition and allow the energy of the crystals to amplify your intuitive abilities. Regular practice, patience, and attunement to your inner guidance will enhance your divination skills and deepen your connection with the crystals.

Chapter 31

Enhancing dreamwork and astral projection using crystals

CRYSTALS CAN PLAY A significant role in enhancing dreamwork and facilitating astral projection experiences. By incorporating specific crystals into your practice, you can amplify your dream recall, promote lucid dreaming, and support astral travel. Here's how you can utilize crystals to enhance your dreamwork and astral projection:

1. Crystal Selection:

- Choose crystals that resonate with the realm of dreams, intuition, and higher consciousness. Amethyst, clear quartz, moonstone, labradorite, and selenite are some crystals commonly associated with dreamwork and astral projection.

- Cleanse and consecrate your chosen crystals by using your preferred method, such as smudging with sage, placing them under the moonlight, or immersing them in a bowl of saltwater. This process helps clear any stagnant energy and attune the crystals to your intentions.

2. Dreamwork:

- Place a crystal under your pillow or near your bedside to enhance dream recall. Amethyst or moonstone is particularly helpful for this purpose.

- Before sleep, hold a crystal in your hand and set the intention to remember your dreams. Visualize the crystal's energy enveloping you with a gentle, protective light.

- Keep a dream journal or notebook by your bed to record your dreams immediately upon waking. Write down any details, emotions, or symbols that stand out to you. Crystals like labradorite or amethyst can be placed near your journal to amplify the energy of your dream reflections.

3. Lucid Dreaming:

- Amethyst is a crystal known for its connection to higher consciousness and spiritual awareness. Place an amethyst crystal under your pillow or hold it in your hand before sleep to encourage lucid dreaming.

- Throughout the day, practice reality checks by asking yourself, "Am I dreaming?" and perform simple tests like trying to push your finger through your palm. The amethyst's energy can help heighten your awareness and improve your ability to recognize when you are dreaming.

4. Astral Projection:

- Create a sacred space for astral projection by placing crystals around your meditation area or bed. Selenite, clear quartz, and amethyst are particularly beneficial for this purpose.

- Prior to your astral projection practice, hold a crystal in your hand and meditate with the intention to connect with higher realms and explore the astral plane.

- Visualize the crystal's energy enveloping you in a protective field as you enter a deep meditative state. Focus on your intention to project your consciousness beyond the physical realm.

- If you use crystals during your astral projection practice, ensure they are cleansed and attuned to your intentions. Consider placing crystals such as amethyst or labradorite near your body or on your astral projection altar.

Remember that the effectiveness of crystals in dreamwork and astral projection is influenced by your intentions, mindset, and consistency of practice. Crystals can act as amplifiers, but the true power lies within you. Trust your intuition, set clear intentions, and explore the depths of your consciousness with the support of these magnificent crystal allies.

Chapter 32

Crystal Spells for Rituals and Sabbats

CRYSTALS CAN ENHANCE THE energy and intention of your rituals and Sabbat celebrations, infusing them with their unique properties and vibrations. Whether you're honoring the cycles of nature, casting spells, or performing specific rituals, incorporating crystals can deepen your connection and amplify the magic. Here are some crystal spells for rituals and Sabbats:

1. Imbolc (February 2nd):

    - Crystal: Amethyst

    - Spell: Place an amethyst crystal on your altar during your Imbolc ritual. Meditate with the crystal, focusing on your intentions for the coming spring season. Visualize the amethyst's energy infusing you with inspiration, creativity, and clarity of mind.

2. Ostara (Spring Equinox, March 20th-23rd):

- Crystal: Green Aventurine

- Spell: Hold a green aventurine crystal in your hand as you welcome the arrival of spring. Visualize the vibrant energy of the crystal merging with the awakening energy of nature. Set your intentions for growth, new beginnings, and balance. Carry the crystal with you throughout the day to maintain a connection with the energy of Ostara.

3. Beltane (May 1st):

- Crystal: Rose Quartz

- Spell: Create a Beltane love spell using rose quartz. Place the crystal in a small cauldron or container filled with fresh flowers and herbs associated with love and passion. Light a candle and visualize the flame igniting the energy of the crystal, amplifying love, and attracting soulful connections. Speak your desires aloud and release the energy into the universe.

4. Litha (Summer Solstice, June 20th-23rd):

- Crystal: Sunstone

- Spell: Hold a sunstone crystal in your hand as you welcome the peak of summer. Stand outside under the sun's rays and let the crystal absorb the solar energy. Visualize the sunstone's vibrant energy filling you with warmth, vitality, and abundance. Set intentions for personal growth, success, and joyful experiences during the summer season.

5. Mabon (Autumn Equinox, September 20th-23rd):

- Crystal: Carnelian

- Spell: Use a carnelian crystal to honor the harvest season. Hold the crystal in your hand and reflect on your personal harvest, acknowledging your accomplishments and expressing gratitude. Place the carnelian on your altar surrounded by autumn leaves and symbols of abundance. Light a candle and give thanks for the blessings in your life.

6. Samhain (October 31st):

- Crystal: Obsidian

- Spell: Connect with the energy of Samhain using obsidian, a crystal associated with protection and psychic abilities. Create an altar dedicated to your ancestors and place the obsidian crystal at the center. Light candles and speak aloud the names of your ancestors, inviting their presence and guidance. Meditate with the obsidian to heighten your psychic awareness and honor the thinning of the veil between realms.

7. Yule (Winter Solstice, December 20th-23rd):

- Crystal: Clear Quartz

- Spell: Embrace the energy of the winter solstice with clear quartz, a crystal of clarity and amplification. Hold a clear quartz crystal in your hand and visualize the rebirth of the sun and the return of light. Set intentions for renewal, inner reflection, and inviting positivity into your life. Place the crystal on your altar or by a window to capture the essence of the returning sunlight.

Remember to cleanse and charge your crystals before each ritual or Sabbat celebration. Use your intuition to select the crystals that resonate with the energy of the occasion and your intentions. By incorporating these crystal spells into

Chapter 33

Incorporating crystals into Wiccan rituals and celebrations

Incorporating crystals into Wiccan rituals and celebrations can enhance the energy, intention, and magic of your practice. Here are some ways you can incorporate crystals into your Wiccan rituals and celebrations:

1. Altar Decorations: Place crystals on your altar as sacred decorations. Choose crystals that resonate with the specific ritual or celebration you are performing. For example, use clear quartz for purification rituals, rose quartz for love rituals, or amethyst for psychic and spiritual rituals. Arrange the crystals in a way that feels aesthetically pleasing and aligned with your intentions.

2. Crystal Grids: Create crystal grids on your altar or sacred space to amplify the energy of your rituals. Select crystals that align with your intentions and arrange them in a geometric pattern. You can use a central crystal to represent your main goal or intention and sur-

round it with supporting crystals. Activate the grid by visualizing energy flowing through the crystals and connecting them to your desired outcome.

3. Crystal Charging: Use crystals to charge ritual items or ingredients. Place the items on a bed of crystals or surround them with crystals overnight to infuse them with the crystal's energy. For example, you can charge water or oils by placing a specific crystal in the container and allowing its energy to permeate the substance.

4. Crystal Meditation: Incorporate crystals into your meditation practice before or during rituals. Hold a crystal in your hand or place it on your body while you meditate to enhance focus, clarity, and spiritual connection. Choose a crystal that aligns with your intention for the ritual or celebration.

5. Crystal Divination: Use crystals for divination purposes during rituals or celebrations. You can create a sacred space for divination by placing specific crystals, such as amethyst or clear quartz, on your divination tools like tarot cards or runes. The crystals can help amplify your intuition and provide clarity and guidance during your divination practice.

6. Crystal Spellwork: Integrate crystals into your spellwork rituals. Select crystals that correspond to the in-

tention of your spell. You can hold the crystals in your hands, place them on your altar, or create a crystal grid as a focal point for the spell. Visualize the energy of the crystals merging with your intention as you cast your spell.

7. Crystal Offerings: Offer crystals as gifts or offerings during rituals or celebrations. Choose crystals that symbolize blessings, abundance, or protection and place them on your altar or in nature as an offering to deities, spirits, or the elements.

Remember to cleanse and charge your crystals regularly to keep their energy clear and aligned. Trust your intuition when selecting crystals and feel free to explore and experiment with different crystals and their properties to find the ones that resonate with you and your specific rituals and celebrations.

Chapter 34

Crystal spells for each of the eight Sabbats in the Wheel of the Year

1. Imbolc (February 2nd):

    Crystal: Amethyst

    Spell: Hold an amethyst crystal in your hand and light a white candle. Reflect on the energy of new beginnings and purification. Visualize any stagnant or negative energy being released and transformed into positive, vibrant energy. Set your intentions for personal growth, inspiration, and creativity in the coming spring season.

2. Ostara (Spring Equinox, March 20th-23rd):

    Crystal: Green Aventurine

    Spell: Place a green aventurine crystal on your altar. Surround it with fresh flowers, symbolizing the renewal of nature. Light a green candle and meditate on the balance between light and dark. Set intentions for growth, abundance, and balance in your life. Visualize the energy of the green aventurine infusing you with vitality and prosperity.

3. Beltane (May 1st):

Crystal: Rose Quartz

Spell: Hold a rose quartz crystal in your hand and sit near a bonfire or candle flame. Reflect on love, passion, and connection. Set intentions for deepening existing relationships or attracting new love. Visualize the energy of the rose quartz radiating love and harmony. Write down your desires and burn the paper in the fire, releasing your intentions to the universe.

4. Litha (Summer Solstice, June 20th-23rd):

Crystal: Sunstone

Spell: Hold a sunstone crystal in your hand and go outside to bask in the sun's rays. Feel the warmth and vitality of the sun energizing you. Set intentions for success, confidence, and personal power. Visualize the energy of the sunstone empowering you to shine brightly in all aspects of your life. Carry the sunstone with you throughout the day to stay connected to its energy.

5. Lammas/Lughnasadh (August 1st):

Crystal: Citrine

Spell: Hold a citrine crystal in your hand and light a yellow candle. Reflect on abundance, gratitude, and the harvest season. Set intentions for prosperity, abundance, and manifestation. Visualize the energy of the citrine attracting opportunities and abundance into your life. Write down your blessings and goals on a piece of paper and place it under the citrine crystal, infusing it with your intentions.

6. Mabon (Autumn Equinox, September 20th-23rd):
   Crystal: Carnelian
   Spell: Hold a carnelian crystal in your hand and sit in nature, surrounded by fallen leaves. Reflect on the balance between light and dark within yourself. Set intentions for inner harmony, gratitude, and balance. Visualize the energy of the carnelian grounding and stabilizing you. Offer a small portion of food or drink to the earth as a symbol of gratitude for the harvest.

7. Samhain (October 31st):
   Crystal: Obsidian
   Spell: Place an obsidian crystal on your altar or in a sacred space. Light a black candle and sit in meditation. Connect with your ancestors and spirit guides, seeking their wisdom and guidance. Set intentions for protection, psychic development, and transformation. Visualize the energy of the obsidian creating a shield of protection around you and opening the gateway to the spirit realm.

8. Yule (Winter Solstice, December 20th-23rd):

Crystal: Clear Quartz

Spell: Hold a clear quartz crystal in your hand and sit in a quiet space. Reflect on the return of light and the rebirth of the sun. Set intentions for clarity, renewal, and spiritual growth. Visualize the energy of the clear quartz purifying and amplifying your intentions. Light a white candle to symbolize the return of light and the power of transformation.

These crystal spells can be performed during the corresponding Sabbats to align your energy with the themes and energies of each season. Remember to cleanse and charge your crystals before use, and trust your intuition when selecting the crystals that resonate with you and your intentions for each Sabbat.

Chapter 35

Aligning with seasonal energies and enhancing magical potency with crystals

CRYSTALS CAN BE POWERFUL allies in aligning with the seasonal energies and enhancing the potency of your magical workings throughout the Wheel of the Year. By selecting crystals that resonate with the specific qualities and energies of each season, you can amplify your intentions and connect more deeply with the natural rhythms of the Earth. Here are some ways to align with seasonal energies and enhance your magical potency using crystals:

1. Spring:

    - Crystal: Green Aventurine or Moss Agate

    - Use these crystals to harness the energy of growth, renewal, and new beginnings that are abundant in spring. Carry them with you during nature walks, meditate with them to cultivate a sense of vitality and fresh perspectives, or incorporate them into spells and rituals focused on personal growth and manifestation.

2. Summer:

- Crystal: Sunstone or Carnelian

- Harness the vibrant energy of the sun and the warmth of summer with these crystals. Use them to ignite passion, confidence, and creativity in your magical workings. Incorporate them into spells and rituals aimed at personal empowerment, success, and abundance.

3. Autumn:

- Crystal: Citrine or Amber

- Embrace the energy of harvest, gratitude, and transformation with these crystals. Use them to amplify intentions related to abundance, manifestation, and releasing old patterns. Place them on your altar or carry them with you as you explore the changing colors of nature and reflect on the blessings in your life.

4. Winter:

- Crystal: Clear Quartz or Snowflake Obsidian

- Connect with the stillness, introspection, and inner transformation of winter using these crystals. Use clear quartz to amplify your intentions and focus your energy during meditation and spellwork. Snowflake obsidian can assist in grounding and releasing negative energies. Carry these crystals with you during winter solstice rituals or use them to infuse your magical workings with clarity and protection.

5. Sabbats:

- Select crystals that resonate with the themes and energies of each Sabbat. For example, use amethyst for Imbolc to invoke inspiration and spiritual growth, or use rose quartz for Beltane to enhance love and passion. Tailor your crystal selection to align with the specific intentions and energies of each Sabbat celebration.

To enhance the magical potency of your crystal work, consider the following practices:

- Cleanse and charge your crystals regularly to ensure their energy is clear and aligned with your intentions.

- Create crystal grids or altars that incorporate seasonal

elements, such as flowers, leaves, or symbols representing the current season or Sabbat.

- Use crystals in combination with other magical tools, such as candles, herbs, or tarot cards, to amplify their energy and create synergistic effects.

- Meditate with your chosen crystals to deepen your connection and attune yourself to the seasonal energies.

- Trust your intuition when selecting crystals, allowing yourself to be drawn to the ones that resonate with your intentions and the energies you wish to align with.

Remember, the key to enhancing magical potency with crystals is to cultivate a strong intention, focus your energy, and work in harmony with the natural rhythms of the seasons.

Chapter 36

Conclusion

In conclusion, "Wicca's Book of Crystal Spells" serves as a comprehensive guide to incorporating crystals into Wiccan practice. Throughout the book, readers are introduced to the fundamental principles of Wicca, the significance of crystals in magical workings, and how to effectively integrate crystals into various aspects of their spiritual journey.

The book offers a wealth of knowledge on understanding crystals in Wicca, including guidance on choosing the right crystals for different intentions and spells, cleansing and charging crystals for optimal spellwork, and the basics of crystal spell crafting. Readers will also learn how to set up sacred spaces, cast circles, invoke elemental energies, and craft and consecrate ritual tools for crystal spells.

The book delves into specific areas of focus, providing crystal spells for love and relationships, protection and cleansing, healing and well-being, abundance and prosperity, divination and intuition, as well as incorporating crystals into Wiccan rituals and celebrations throughout the Wheel of the Year.

Readers will discover how to attract love, heal troubled relationships, strengthen bonds, protect their homes, clear negative energies, enhance physical and emotional well-being, manifest abundance, develop psychic abilities, and connect with higher consciousness using the power of crystals.

By aligning with seasonal energies and utilizing crystals, readers can enhance the potency of their magical workings and deepen their connection to the natural rhythms of the Earth. The book provides practical tips and step-by-step instructions to guide readers in incorporating crystals into their magical practices, empowering them to create their own rituals, spells, and sacred spaces.

"Wicca's Book of Crystal Spells" invites readers to explore the beautiful synergy between Wicca and crystal magic, offering a wealth of knowledge and inspiration to support their spiritual journey. Whether you are a beginner or an experienced practitioner, this book is a valuable resource that will enrich your understanding of crystals and their transformative power in Wiccan practice. Embrace the magic of crystals and unlock the limitless possibilities they hold for your spiritual growth and empowerment.

Chapter 37

Recap of the importance of crystal spells in Wicca

IN WICCA, CRYSTAL SPELLS hold great importance and are widely utilized in magical workings. Crystals are seen as powerful tools that can enhance and amplify intentions, connect with elemental energies, and create a deeper connection with the divine. Here's a recap of the importance of crystal spells in Wicca:

1. Amplifying Intentions: Crystals have unique energetic properties that can magnify and focus intentions. By selecting the right crystals for specific purposes, Wiccans can intensify their spells and rituals, enhancing the likelihood of desired outcomes.

2. Connecting with Elemental Energies: Crystals are associated with different elements such as earth, air, fire, and water. By incorporating specific crystals aligned with these elements, Wiccans can tap into their corresponding energies, creating a harmonious balance and amplifying the magical work.

3. Facilitating Spiritual Growth: Crystals are believed to possess their own consciousness and wisdom. Working with crystals can help Wiccans deepen their spiritual connection, expand their intuition, and accelerate personal growth. Crystals can also aid in opening pathways to higher realms of consciousness and divine guidance.

4. Cleansing and Purifying: Crystals have the ability to absorb and transmute negative energies, making them valuable tools for cleansing and purifying both individuals and spaces. By incorporating crystals into rituals or using them for energy clearing, Wiccans can create a harmonious and sacred environment for their magical workings.

5. Balancing and Harmonizing Energies: Different crystals possess unique vibrational frequencies that can help restore balance and harmony to one's energetic body. By working with crystals, Wiccans can address imbalances, heal emotional wounds, and restore equilibrium, leading to overall well-being.

6. Enhancing Intuition and Divination: Crystals can heighten psychic abilities and facilitate intuitive insights. Wiccans often use crystals for divination purposes, such as scrying or pendulum work, to gain clarity, guidance, and a deeper understanding of the spiritual realms.

7. Connecting with Nature: Crystals are gifts from the Earth, and their use in Wiccan practice reinforces the connection to nature and the cycles of the natural world. By incorporating crystals into rituals and spells, Wiccans honor the Earth and harness its energies in its magical workings.

By recognizing the importance of crystal spells in Wicca and understanding their unique properties and energies, practitioners can harness the transformative power of crystals to amplify their magical intentions, deepen their spiritual practice, and create profound shifts in their lives.

Chapter 38

Encouragement for readers to explore and experiment with their own crystal magic

In "Wicca's Book of Crystal Spells," we encourage readers to embark on their own journey of exploration and experimentation with crystal magic. While the book provides a solid foundation and a wide range of spells and practices, it's important to remember that your personal connection and intuition are key in harnessing the full potential of crystal magic. Here's an encouragement for readers to explore and experiment with their own crystal magic:

1. Trust Your Intuition: Each person has a unique energetic resonance and connection with crystals. Trust your intuition when selecting crystals for your spells and rituals. Allow yourself to be drawn to the crystals that resonate with you on a deep level, even if they may not be traditionally associated with a particular intention. Your intuition will guide you to the crystals that are most aligned with your energy and the specific needs

of your magical workings.

2. Experiment with Different Combinations: Don't be afraid to mix and match crystals to create your own combinations. Just as different herbs and spices blend together to create unique flavors, crystals can synergize their energies when used together. Explore different crystal pairings and observe how their energies interact and amplify each other. This experimentation allows you to uncover new possibilities and discover your own personalized crystal rituals.

3. Record and Reflect: Keep a journal of your crystal magic experiences. Record the crystals you use, the intentions you set, and the outcomes you observe. Reflect on how different crystals affect your energy, mood, and overall well-being. This record will serve as a valuable resource for future reference and will help you identify patterns, preferences, and any unique associations you establish with specific crystals.

4. Personalize Your Rituals: While the book provides a variety of crystal spells, feel free to personalize and adapt them to suit your needs and beliefs. Incorporate symbols, elements, and rituals that resonate with your personal spiritual path. Infuse your own intentions, chants, and visualizations into your crystal spells. Your own personal touch will make the magic more mean-

ingful and powerful for you.

5. Embrace the Unexpected: Remember that magic works in mysterious ways, and sometimes the most powerful transformations come from unexpected sources. Be open to surprises and be willing to let the energy of the crystals guide you. Be curious and receptive to the messages and synchronicities that arise as you work with crystals. Embrace the journey and trust that the crystals will support and guide you on your path.

By exploring and experimenting with your own crystal magic, you are tapping into your own innate power as a magical practitioner. Allow your curiosity to guide you, take risks, and step outside of your comfort zone. The world of crystals is vast and ever-evolving, offering endless possibilities for growth, healing, and spiritual expansion. Embrace the adventure, and let your own unique crystal magic unfold.

Chapter 39

Final thoughts on the transformative power of crystals in spiritual practice

IN CONCLUSION, THE TRANSFORMATIVE power of crystals in spiritual practice is awe-inspiring and profound. Crystals have been revered for centuries for their ability to harness and amplify energy, connect us with the natural world, and facilitate spiritual growth. Their unique energetic properties and sacred beauty make them powerful tools for personal transformation and the manifestation of our intentions.

When we work with crystals in our spiritual practice, we enter into a co-creative dance with the Earth and the universe. Crystals serve as conduits of divine energy, helping us align our intentions with higher frequencies and tap into the wisdom of the universe. They can enhance our intuition, deepen our connection with our higher selves, and awaken dormant spiritual abilities.

Crystals have the remarkable capacity to heal and restore balance on all levels—physical, emotional, mental, and spiritual. They can help us release old patterns, heal emotional wounds, and bring about profound shifts in our consciousness. Through their subtle vibrations, crystals harmonize our energetic bodies, uplift our spirits, and support our overall well-being.

The transformative power of crystals extends beyond our individual journeys. They also have the potential to create collective change and influence the world around us. When we infuse our intentions for love, healing, and peace into our crystal work, we contribute to the greater collective consciousness and the well-being of the planet.

It is important to approach our relationship with crystals with respect, gratitude, and reverence. As we work with crystals, we become caretakers of these precious gifts from the Earth. By honoring their energy, cleansing and charging them regularly, and working with them consciously, we deepen our connection to the Earth and the spiritual realms.

Remember that the true power of crystals lies within you. While crystals can enhance our spiritual practice and support our intentions, it is our intention, focus, and belief that ultimately shape the magic. Trust your intuition, follow your heart, and allow the transformative energy of crystals to guide you on your spiritual journey.

As you delve into the world of crystal magic, may you discover the depths of your own power and wisdom. Embrace the beauty, mystery, and transformative power of crystals in your spiritual practice. May they illuminate your path, awaken your spirit, and bring blessings into every aspect of your life.

www.ingramcontent.com/pod-product-compliance
Lightning Source LLC
Chambersburg PA
CBHW072021060426
42449CB00033B/1516